How to Chat Someone Up at a Funeral

How to Chat Someone Up at a Funeral

And Other Awkward
Social Situations

Mark Leigh

JOHN BLAKE

Published by John Blake Publishing Ltd,
3 Bramber Court, 2 Bramber Road,
London W14 9PB, England

www.johnblakepublishing.co.uk
www.facebook.com/johnblakebooks 🅵
twitter.com/jblakebooks 🆃

This edition published in 2014

ISBN: 978-1-78418-017-1

British Library Cataloguing-in-Publication Data:

A catalogue record for this book is available from the British Library.

Design by www.envydesign.co.uk

Illustrations by Karen Donnelly

Printed in Great Britain by CPI Group (UK) Ltd

1 3 5 7 9 10 8 6 4 2

Papers used by John Blake Publishing are natural, recyclable products made from
wood grown in sustainable forests. The manufacturing processes conform to the
environmental regulations of the country of origin.

Every attempt has been made to contact the relevant copyright-holders,
but some were unobtainable. We would be grateful if the appropriate
people could contact us.

WARNING!

If you rely solely on the advice given in this book to get you out of any of the specific life-threatening situations covered, you're an idiot and, quite frankly, you deserve everything you get. The information, hints and tips are for guidance only and the author and publishers disclaim any liability from any injury resulting from the use of the information contained in this book, including (but not limited to) being mauled by a grizzly bear, maimed by a co-worker, bitten by a zombie, slapped by a pregnant woman, beaten up by a meth dealer or probed by aliens. So there!

ABOUT THE AUTHOR

Mark Leigh has managed to find himself in more awkward social situations than he cares to remember (most of his own doing) and can always be relied upon to say or do the wrong thing in any given circumstance. He is particularly uncomfortable in the presence of people, animals and inanimate objects.

When he's not trying to extricate himself from embarrassing incidents Mark has somehow found the time to write or co-write fifty humour and trivia books on subjects as diverse as celebrities, extra-terrestrials, swearing pets and toilets.

Mark lives in Surrey with his family and dog and when he's not writing or feeling awkward, steals pens and photocopier paper from his job in marketing. For more details visit www.mark-leigh.com

Contents

Introduction

Awkward social situations come in many shapes and forms. There are those everyday circumstances where saying or doing the wrong thing will upset people or make you look stupid. Then there are those more extreme scenarios where an inappropriate response or action could lead to actual injury or death.

The aim of this book therefore is to offer you the essential help and advice to deal with a wide spectrum of social situations so you don't end up either as a social pariah or a corpse, or something in between.

Virtually all of the advice and guidance contained within these pages is drawn from my own personal observations and experiences – and the perilous and sometimes terrifying process of trial and error. Unlike you, I had to learn the hard way. There were no books to tell me the right way to behave at a swingers' party or an exorcism; advising me how to deal with an office affair or compose a ransom note, or setting out the rules that apply to flat sharing with a silverback gorilla or negotiating with a pimp.

So, benefit from my own experience and heed my advice, hints and tips for dealing with a whole host of awkward social situations from challenging a co-worker to a duel or haggling when buying crystal meth, to accidentally wearing Nazi uniform to your niece's wedding or making your escape from a mountain lion at a dinner party.

Of course, there are a few scenarios I haven't experienced such as coping with a Zombie attack, dating a werewolf or knowing the right thing to wear in a post apocalypse world, however the advice I offer is based on my own acute and respected insights into these scenarios.

So, dear reader, have faith; put your best foot forward and keep it away from your mouth. Remember, I've been shunned, slapped, sacked, mauled, maimed, dumped, sued, probed and imprisoned so you don't have to be.

Mark Leigh
Surrey, England 2014

Inadvertently farting in the presence of the Queen

Contrary to popular belief, farting in the presence of The Queen does not constitute high treason and is therefore not punishable by life imprisonment in the Tower of London. However, in spite of this act being considered a lesser offence it is still essential to apologise and to be aware of the accepted etiquette when doing so.

THE CORRECT PROTOCOL

1. Always address The Queen as 'Your Majesty', and subsequently 'ma'am' (to rhyme with Pam).
2. The apology should leave The Queen in no doubt that your fart was accidental and as far as humanly possible, completely out of your control. Never, ever admit it was a deliberate act undertaken as some sort of political or social comment – or for a wager.
3. Never use the word 'fart' or 'farting'; the use of these terms is considered a sign of ill breeding. Appropriate

*Never attempt
to blame your
flatulence on one
of the royal corgis.*

terms are 'passing wind' or 'flatulence'. However, in certain circumstances euphemisms including – but not limited to – the following may be used: 'guffing', 'playing Satan's bugle', 'crop dusting', 'firing a stink torpedo', 'trouser trumpet', 'knicker-ripper' and 'making the call of the barking spider'.

4. Never attempt to blame your flatulence on one of the royal corgis, or The Duchess of Cambridge. The Queen has heard it all before.

5. After The Queen has responded to your apology, you should leave her company by making a small bow or curtsy. Although it will probably have good comedic effect, resist the temptation to fart again while undertaking these actions.

6. Her Majesty fails to find any humour whatsoever in someone farting after immediately saying, 'Hey Queenie, pull my finger'.

7. Likewise, the royal funny bone will not be tickled if you say, 'Hey Maj, better out than in!'

SAMPLE APOLOGIES

- 'I am very sorry, Your Majesty, for playing Satan's bugle in your direction. I underestimated the effect of the sauerkraut and cauliflower served at the state banquet.'
- 'Your Majesty, I apologise for my vapour caper; this malodorous whiff was the result of the curse of irritable bowel syndrome.'
- 'Ma'am, I express my sincerest regret for cutting the cheese at the exact moment you knighted me. I can only put this down to a combination of anxiety, excitement and an earlier bowl of All-Bran.'

Disarming an axe-wielding maniac

When confronting an axe wielding maniac, or indeed a maniac of any sort, it is important to note that their mental state means their behaviour is likely to be very unpredictable. Despite this, if you are unarmed yourself there are still some basic techniques you can use to minimise the threat and degree of injury that is likely to be inflicted.

HOW TO AVOID MUTILATION AND/OR DEATH

Rule 1: Acknowledge that you are likely to get hurt
This could be anything from a graze or minor cut (unlikely) to the loss of one or more limbs or a very painful and bloody death (highly probable). Conceding that serious injury is a likely possibility will improve your own psychological state and ability to fight back.

Rule 2: Do not run away from the maniac – get closer to them
This might seem absurd, almost imbecilic, unbelievably senseless

and catastrophically dangerous advice when your natural reaction will be to run away as fast as you can. However, space between you and the maniac works to his/her advantage, giving them room to manoeuvre the axe.

Rule 3: Quickly read the intent of the maniac

Do they want your money, your mobile phone, your car or your partner – or do they just want to maim or kill you for no apparent reason? If you can, buy your way out of the situation by offering material possessions or try reasoning. If the maniac is intent on violence just for the sake of it (as 95 per cent of them are), be prepared to fight back with all your might.

Rule 4: Do not try to intercept the axe

Trying to focus on the axe is the most serious mistake you can make (apart from getting yourself in this situation in the first place). Your objective must be to stop the maniac, not the inanimate yet very sharp object in his or her hand.

Rule 5: Attack the limb controlling the axe

The initial most-practical attack will be to land a blow on the maniac's forearm (Note: ensure this is the forearm holding the axe). The second most-practical attack will be to aim for their upper arm or shoulder. Striking any of these should allow you to momentarily divert the attack or even (although very unlikely) disarm the maniac.

Rule 6: Destroy the maniac's central senses

Your final goal should be an attack to the maniac's head or neck to either control their body or render them unconscious. A headlock or chokehold is suitable until (or if) help arrives.

3

Bribing a foreign border guard

You know how it is: all you want to do is cross from Nigeria to Chad or from Guatemala to El Salvador. The border guards have inspected your passport and with a look that's as predictable as it is unnerving, shake their heads and tell you that there seems to be some sort of 'problem'.

They don't usually elaborate on what the so-called issue is – but that's not important. All you need to know is that like most problems, there's always a solution; in this case it's greasing the palms of officialdom.

Border guards are known as much for their greed as their intransigence, so if you're naive or decide to take the moral high ground, be prepared for a very long wait at the crossing or airport until you change your mind or your travel plans. If, on the other hand, you acknowledge that bribery is one of the three defining characteristics of a developing nation (along with flies and child labour), then it's important to recognise that corruption has its own elaborate etiquette.

The following system of unwritten rules and procedures has

been established to avoid detection and to make the transaction as smooth and as quick as possible.

HOW TO SUCCESSFULLY GREASE THE PALMS OF FOREIGN OFFICIALDOM

Rule 1: Let them take the first step
Even though you might expect to pay a bribe, don't offer payment before the official has made his/her intentions clear. Doing so is considered the height of bad manners.

Rule 2: Recognise the euphemisms
Despite having questionable ethics, most corrupt border police still pride themselves on having a certain dignity and won't resort to blatantly asking for money outright to stamp your documentation. Instead they'll ask you to pay an 'expediting payment', a 'processing fee', or 'expenses'. Other times they may ask you for a 'small gift' or suggest you 'discuss the matter over tea' then wink at you or stamp one foot. These are all well-worn euphemisms.
Note: The universal sign of an official rubbing his/her thumb and forefinger together can overcome any language barriers.

Rule 3: Let them name their price first
This simple rule prevents you overpaying. In some impoverished countries you can get away with a packet of cigarettes, in others, just two Silk Cut. In others, you can gain free passage just by handing over a biro or a packet of Juicy Fruit.

Rule 4: Negotiating your bribe (optional)
In most cases, border officials think every foreigner visiting their country drives a Rolls-Royce and lives in a mansion with

a butler called Hudson. They will always name a price far more than they want, so it's your prerogative whether to pay this or enter into what could be protracted bargaining.

Note: Negotiating a bribe isn't like haggling for a knock-off designer bag or T-shirt in a market. Firstly, you can't just walk away if you're unhappy with the price, and secondly, the people you're haggling with usually have a very short attention span, no sense of humour and carry a gun.

Rule 5: Be discrete

Although bribery nearly always involves the physical handing of money from one party to another, corruption etiquette states that the cash must be hidden from view. Handing a border guard a wad of notes, while acceptable, is considered vulgar and tactless. Bribes should be hidden inside passports, airline ticket wallets, travel itineraries or, of course, brown (never white) envelopes.

Rule 6: Never ask for a receipt

In conclusion

Don't let the existence and expectation of bribery dissuade you from visiting foreign countries. To ensure you experience trouble-free travel, make sure you follow the rules above and remember, it's a jungle out there!

Note: Native guides will often need bribing to ensure your safe passage out of a jungle.

4

Challenging a co-worker to a duel

Playing the radio too loud... messing with the room thermostat... pushing your stapler over the desk boundary line... High-pressure work environments are often the breeding grounds for petty disagreements to rapidly develop into full-scale disruptive arguments and even accusations of misconduct or discrimination. Managers are keen to resolve any such issues by a formal arbitration process. However, challenging your co-worker to a duel can be a far more effective way of settling such disputes.

THE ADVANTAGES OF A DUEL OVER AN EMPLOYMENT TRIBUNAL

• Employment tribunals are bogged down by the need to adhere to formal procedures and practices and usually involve lengthy and dull discussions in the Small Meeting

Settling inter-office disputes via a duel can be more satisfying than a formal arbitration process.

Room. A duel can simply involve swords or pistols and a corridor.

- An employment tribunal has rules and is associated with bureaucracy; a duel follows a code and is associated with honour.
- Winning an employment tribunal does not give you anywhere near the same satisfaction as piercing your co-worker's heart with a rapier.

Note: If the idea of duel is appealing, please check it is permitted under your contract of employment. You'll usually find the subject covered in the company handbook somewhere near the notes on dress code and holiday entitlement.

DUELLING: THE CODE

Remember that a duel is not an impromptu scuffle or brawl. It's a pre-arranged and controlled fight between men or women of honour and as such, a certain degree of dignity is expected from both parties by adhering to the code.

1. Duels don't happen spontaneously; a challenge must first be issued to your opponent. Historically this consisted of throwing a glove or a gauntlet on to the ground in front of them. These days, email is an acceptable alternative.
2. The challenger must clearly state his/her reason for the duel. This can take the form of an attached Word document or, if the reasons are more complicated, a PowerPoint presentation using clip art or animation may be used to give a more detailed explanation of the grievance.

3. Once the challenge is explained and issued, a specified time and place for the duel must be agreed. Using Microsoft Outlook is recommended to invite your opponent and ensure both parties have a clear record of the event. Accepting the meeting is taken as your official recognition of the duel and its consequences.

4. The person challenged has the right to choose the weapon. Traditionally this will be a sword or pistol. Throwing plant pots or even reams of A4 photocopier paper at your opponent, while acceptable, does not uphold the true spirit of the duel.

5. Ensure the selected venue has sufficient space for the duel to take place. Low suspended ceilings can seriously hinder a sword fight while pistols fired in the car park are likely to cause collateral damage, including the MD's Range Rover or a random group of smokers.

6. Both parties have the right to appoint a 'second'. Their role is to prepare the weapons and make sure the rules of the duel are followed. Your second can be anyone in the company: the maintenance guy, the posh bird in marketing or even that creepy bloke in accounts.

7. The winner of the duel is whoever has scored first blood. This does not necessarily mean death; it could be a nick from a sword, a wound from a bullet or if stationery is thrown, a paper cut.

8. The loser must concede defeat and accept inevitable humiliation in the company newsletter.

5

How to dump someone, yet still look like you care

It's never easy to break up with someone and it's even less comfortable saying '*sayonara*' in person. Text and email goodbyes are cowardly while just changing your Facebook status to 'Single' is considered the height of bad manners. Letter writing, although more thoughtful, tends to be a lost and almost arcane art.

The best solution by far is using the traditional Japanese poetic form haiku, a win–win situation in just three lines. Working within its strict regime of seventeen syllables over three lines forces you to be clear and concise. There's no room for mixed messages. Plus, the fact you've adopted this historic poetic form indicates to your ex-partner that you're sensitive and you still care... the split is therefore far more palatable.

EXAMPLES OF HAIKU BREAK-UP POETRY

Our love has faded
Blameless; all you did was right
It's not you. It's me.

Words choke in my throat
You deserve someone better
(I know that I do).

Sorry I'm leaving
I got off with your bezzie
Didn't she tell you?

It's different now
It's true, I do still love you
But like a brother.

They say breaking up
Is hard to do. No, it's not.
Don't ever call me.

So sad, our parting
If only you had managed
To lose thirty pounds.

16

I found all those texts
The ones you sent to that skank
Now you're deleted.

You cheating slimeball!
I moved out and took the cat
She hates you as well.

SEE ALSO: Composing a 'Dear John' letter, p.252

6

Getting an erection while making a presentation at work

Men are genetically predisposed to be aroused by visual and mental stimulation. Add to that the risks of chafing from underwear and you'll understand why erections can occur at the most inappropriate times and locations. Research has shown that the most embarrassing and awkward time to have an erection is standing up, making a presentation in front of colleagues or clients. Unless you're talking about the third quarter's Viagra sales and are trying to emphasise a point, it's often difficult to explain why there's a significant bulge in your trousers as you click through your PowerPoint slides.

If this situation arises, never, under any circumstances, attempt to explain or even justify what has happened. Instead, deal with the situation by concealment or some form of forced detumescence.

Be as discrete as possible when concealing a telltale trouser bulge.

THE 10 MOST EMBARRASSING OCCASIONS TO HAVE AN ERECTION

- Making a presentation at work
- Public speaking
- Dancing with your daughter at her wedding
- At a petting zoo
- Working as a department store Santa
- Standing on a diving board
- Being patted down during airport security
- Watching *The Little Mermaid*
- Performing a post-mortem
- In a bar, riding a mechanical bull

Source: Midwest Institute for Erectile Studies, Chicago

HOW TO DEAL WITH AN INOPPORTUNE ERECTION

Wear loose clothing

If you're susceptible to involuntary erections, dress accordingly as a precaution. The most obvious clothing is a baggy suit; however, also consider a loose ankle-length Arabic gown, a poncho or toga. If challenged over your ethnic dress style respond that you wanted to embrace your company's support of multiculturalism in the workplace... or you thought it was Kaftan Tuesday.

Think unsexy thoughts

You wouldn't associate a discussion about the new sales strategy for pasta shapes with any form of sexual stimulation; however, for some men the thought of a new product launch, distribution channels or even spaghetti is enough to send blood rushing to the groin. To minimise any chance of arousal it's best to think completely unsexy thoughts before it's your turn to take centre stage. Topics include: the Rwandan genocide, mustard, your credit card bill, gum disease, a barbed-wire catheter, your granny wearing a bikini, kittens in a blender, your granny in a blender.

Distract yourself

If you have problems with any of the above (for example, you actually find the image of your bikini-clad granny a turn-on), then try and solve a difficult mental mathematical problem. For example, think of the first twenty numbers in the Fibonacci series, or count to 100 in binary.

Concealment

For many, this is the obvious solution if giving a presentation at work. An A4 pad strategically held in front of the groin can discreetly disguise any inappropriate bulges; however, it's best to hold this naturally in just one hand as you address your audience. Holding it in two hands will simply draw attention to the area. Alternatively, if you find yourself without props, just clasp both hands in front of your groin and keep them there. Presenting like this while speaking slowly will make your audience think you're a distinguished gentleman with something important to say.

Mis-direction

Waving your arms around and gesticulating like a southern Italian while presenting has the dual benefit of making it seem that you're passionate about your subject, while drawing unwanted attention away from your groin.

Hands in pockets

It is sometimes possible to suppress your erection by careful manoeuvring it with one or both hands in your trouser pockets; the downside is that giving a presentation or speech in this way can also make you look too casual or overconfident. In both senses of the word, be careful not to appear too cocky.

Walking around

Walking makes the blood circulate more and, in theory, drain from your groin into other extremities like your arms and legs. However, movement can also cause friction from underwear, which may prolong your erection. A high-risk strategy.

Hold something cold

Cold sends blood away from your extremities into the body's core, causing your erection to fade. With practice it can become second nature to hold a glass of cold water against your groin without looking as though you're sipping through your fly.

Hold your breath

Doing this for a prolonged period will divert blood to your brain, reducing the erection in a very short space of time. The downside is that you'll look like you're holding your breath. If challenged afterwards, claim it's a breathing exercise. Should you be challenged again, say that you meant it was a non-breathing exercise.

7

Receiving a tarantula as a Secret Santa present

The sparkling wine is flowing and the Lidl own-brand mince pies are fast disappearing. Someone announces it's time for the office Secret Santa and moments later a box of hastily wrapped presents is dragged out from under the over-decorated tree. Expectations are low but merriment is high as the packages are distributed.

Angela from accounts gets that 'Grow Your Own Boyfriend' kit, Pam from sales has the 'Save Water Drink Champagne' towel while Toby in HR receives a novelty iPhone case that makes it look like he has a giant ear when he's making a call. Hilarity ensues then it's your turn to open a gift. It's a small box that rattles as you shake it. You rip off the paper and as you open the lid an angry tarantula scuttles up your arm and takes residence on the side of your face.

Laughter turns to screams. Angela faints. You're rooted to the spot… This is how to deal with it.

PROS AND CONS OF GETTING A TARANTULA AS YOUR OFFICE SECRET SANTA PRESENT

Cons
• While not fatal, tarantula bites can be extremely painful and may cause dangerous allergic reactions in some victims including (but not limited to) profuse swelling, blurred vision, dizziness, difficulty in swallowing, disorientation and breathing difficulties.
• Whatever your workplace achievements, you'll always be known as 'that guy/girl who got bitten by the tarantula'.

Pros
• If bitten, you're unlikely to die.
• Getting a tarantula as a gift saves you from receiving a present that is at least two of the following: a) humiliating, b) cheap, c) thoughtless, d) irrelevant.
• If you're going to get bitten by a tarantula it's better for it to happen in an office than in the middle of the outback or a rainforest.

WHAT TO DO

The first course of action is to brush the tarantula off your face
There are many options available in an office: you could use a ruler, a Sharpie, an A4 pad or a rolled-up copy of the *Sun*. Tarantulas are easily spooked and even a slight nudge will cause them to release their grip; that or bite you.

If the tarantula refuses to be brushed off or there's no implement to hand
Stand up slowly and gently bob up and down. The tarantula will either fall on to the floor or drop down your open shirt or blouse.

Capture the tarantula
As soon as the spider falls on to the floor it is vital it's captured so that it can't bite anyone else. Offices are replete with hilarious mugs proclaiming: 'Don't ask me, I only work here' and 'My job is top secret. Even I don't know what I'm doing', and one of these upturned over the spider will secure it until an animal welfare organisation can be called.
Note: If no one wants their mug to be used you can also drop a ream of 80gsm photocopier paper on to the spider.

IF YOU'RE BITTEN
If you feel one bite you're probably OK. This is called a 'dry bite'. If you're bitten again you should worry; it's this second bite that injects the venom.

In either case, wash the wound, dab it dry and then apply copious amounts of antiseptic cream from the office first aid box; if available also take/apply antihistamine tablets/cream. Seek medical attention as soon as possible.

Ensure you fill in the Accident Book.

8

Assuming someone is pregnant when they're not...

Y ou're on a crowded bus or train and there's a large woman standing near you looking very uncomfortable. Do you perform a selfless act of chivalry and give up your seat or risk upsetting her when it turns out she isn't actually seven months pregnant, just obese?

Comedian Jimmy Carr summed up the dilemma perfectly when he said, 'I'd much rather see a pregnant woman standing up on a bus, than a fat girl sitting down, crying.'

To avoid any embarrassment the best advice is *never* to give up your seat unless you are absolutely, positively certain the woman is pregnant.

These are a few telltale signs that help distinguish between fat and a foetus…

HOW TO SPOT A PREGNANT WOMAN ON PUBLIC TRANSPORT

	Pregnant woman	**Fat woman**
What they're probably eating	Pickle-flavour ice cream; chicken and apple-sauce sandwiches; coal	Big bars of chocolate; a tray of tiramisu; a bucket of KFC; a bucket of any other food
What their badge might say	'Baby on Board'	'I Love Food'
What they're probably reading	Anything with these words in the title: 'Pregnancy', 'Baby', 'Expecting', 'Motherhood', 'Joy'	Anything with this word in the title: 'Diet'
Cause of sickness	Mornings	Overeating
Facial appearance	Rosy glow	Stuffed with crisps
What they're usually talking about	The second trimester; dilation; placenta; amniotic fluid	Pies
What they reply when you ask, 'What are you hoping for?'	'It doesn't matter as long as it's healthy'	'Lunch'

FIVE THINGS TO DO IF YOU'RE TOLD, 'I'M NOT PREGNANT!'

1. Turn the insult into a compliment

'I was looking at your face and you have such a healthy glow. It must be because you're in love.'

OR

'It's just that so many young, beautiful women like yourself are pregnant these days.'

2. Turn the insult into a proposition

'Well, do you want to be?'

3. Divert the blame

Turn to the person standing nearest to you and say. 'See, I told you she wasn't!'

4. Prepare to be slapped

5. Run like hell

If in any doubt whatsoever ...

There are two surefire ways you can be certain a women is pregnant
1. She says she is.
2. You see the baby's head crowning.

9

How to escape from a mountain lion at a dinner party

Mountain lions, also called cougars, tend to be attracted to dinner parties by the aroma of food – not by stimulating conversation about a week in Tuscany, home extensions or the spiralling cost of private education A home invasion by one of these wild cats is considered a social faux pas on a par with mistakenly serving a crisp Zinfandel with roast rack of lamb; however, the outcome will usually be more serious. Offering an inappropriate wine to your guests usually only leads to acute embarrassment, while a cougar running amok in your dining room is likely to result in, at the very least, damaged furniture, and at most, a mauling that results in life-changing injuries or agonising death.

A home invasion by a wild cat is viewed as a considerable social faux pas.

TO SURVIVE A POTENTIAL ATTACK IT IS ESSENTIAL YOU FOLLOW THESE ESSENTIAL DOS AND DON'TS

1. Don't panic

The sight of a cougar crouching on a table that was just moments ago covered with plates of baked lobster tails *can* be alarming. Stay calm and remain still. Your first thought should be to plan an escape route. Dwelling on the likelihood that the cougar will inflict its characteristic killing bite to the back of your neck is likely to cause you to freeze, a situation that will hinder rapid flight.

2. Don't run

The cougar will have already seen and smelt you and running is likely to cause it to pay you more attention and realise that a 68kg (150lb) guest is far more tasty than a summer berry pavlova. However, running can be effective if all guests do it simultaneously (see point 5)

3. Do everything you can to appear larger

Cougars are less likely to attack larger animals. You can appear larger by opening your jacket wide, standing on tiptoes and holding your hands above your head, or by picking up a small sleepy child who wandered downstairs moments before.
Note: The child should be lifted to shoulder height in order to increase your apparent mass, not to throw as a decoy.

4. Do throw things

If you do not have access to jackets or small children (see above), throwing things at the cougar will send the message that you are not prey and in fact might actually be dangerous yourself. Although your choice of objects will be limited in a dinner party scenario, the following have been used with some-times effective results: novelty place settings, decorative napkin holders, tea lights, condiment sets, bottles of extra virgin olive oil and dishes of wholegrain honey mustard.

5. Do run into a secure room simultaneously

The sight and commotion of all its potential victims running into another room at the same time is likely to disorientate the cougar and momentarily confuse it – giving you precious seconds to escape, or at least sacrifice the slowest guests. Once in a safe room, call the authorities or alert neighbours to your predicament.

6. Do apologise to your guests immediately after the event

A simple note should be sent at the earliest opportunity apologising for the interruption and offering a choice of new dates to re-host the party.

10

Negotiating with a pimp

For many men, negotiating with a prostitute can be daunting – unnerving even. For most it's the feeling of acute shame or embarrassment; for others it's the anxiety of being recognised parked at the kerbside or standing uneasily on a street corner. That's why, despite the fact that on average you can expect to pay approximately 50 per cent more for services, it's usually better dealing directly with a pimp.

Negotiating with a pimp requires a different skill set from most other negotiations:
1. Pimps have a very short attention span. The longer they spend haggling the less time their girls are earning – and the more likely you'll piss them off.
2. They are handy with a blade.

WHY IT'S BETTER TO NEGOTIATE WITH A PIMP THAN A HO:

• There's slightly less stigma attached to being seen in an alley talking to a weasly-looking low-life wearing a purple fur coat and carrying a diamond-tipped cane than a cocaine-addled skank wearing a push-up bra, hot pants and torn fishnet stockings.

• The special pimp/ho relationship (usually involving narcotics and/or threatening behaviour) ensures your requirements are met. Dealing direct with a ho leaves you open to being hustled; paying for additional activities that you thought were included.

• Pimps understand that it's easier to retain a client than find a new one, so they only represent girls who meet their exacting standards. This endorsement means it's less awkward than having to ask a ho for a reference.

• Negotiating with the pimp as middleman makes it more of a business transaction and so legitimises the whole process. Or that's what you tell yourself.

TIPS FOR NEGOTIATING

• Ensure the pimp understands everything you want from his ho, i.e. the specific acts required, clothing to be worn/not worn and the duration of the session. Explicitly covering these details upfront will help to avoid misunderstandings with the sex worker (for example, who's doing the peeing and who's being peed on). This sort of confusion can at best lead to disappointment or, at worst, loud screaming.

- Ensure you completely understand any slang being used. To avoid loss of face or credibility, many men pretend they understand pimp slang and are conned into paying extra for certain acts that sound salacious but are just very disappointing. For example, 'spanking the puppy' simply involves corporal punishment administered to a young dog, while 'licking the glazed doughnut' is exactly that.

11

Inadvertently lacing canapes with arsenic

Research has shown that apart from running out of hors d'oeuvres, glacé cherries or ice, accidentally adding arsenic to a plate of canapés is one of the biggest fears of those organising cocktail parties. Nothing says 'I'm an irresponsible hostess' more than the sight of one of her guests collapsing and dying on the floor right next to the vodka luge.

In order to react appropriately to the situation, it's important to recognise the signs that a guest might be affected:

SYMPTOMS OF ARSENIC POISONING
- Stomach cramps
- Hallucinations
- Convulsions
- Severe diarrhoea
- Blood in urine
- Death

If you do suspect you've inadvertently added arsenic to your canapés, follow these simple steps...

1. Keep calm

The first thing to remember is that a good hostess stays cool at all times. Think of the time when someone spilt that raspberry mojito on your white carpet or when Binkie wore that exact same asymmetrical wrap dress. You didn't panic then and you mustn't now.

2. Confirm whether the canapés are affected

Arsenic has the distinctive smell of bitter almonds so detecting this odour will indicate that your canapés do in fact contain arsenic. Or almonds.

3. Make excuses

If you sense that the canapés have been tainted, make excuses for why your guests might be convulsing or lying comatose on the floor. For example, point at them, roll your eyes and mime taking a swig from a bottle. Alternatively, shake your head and say something like, 'She told me she was off street methadone.'

4. Remove bodies

One sure-fire way of ruining a cocktail party is being forced to step over someone to get to the ice. Remove the affected guest as soon as possible and put them somewhere out of sight – for example, in the room reserved for coats or gifts.

5. Administer an antidote

A good hostess will always have a well-stocked first aid kit to hand. Ideally this will contain dimercaprol or dimercaptosuccinic acid, which should be administered intravenously to the guest at the earliest opportunity.

6. Call for an ambulance

Ask the ambulance crew to be discrete when they arrive. Flashing lights and sirens can easily compromise a party atmosphere.

7. Make light of the situation

Your guests will be in party mood and dwelling on the incident could well ruin their enjoyment. A passing comment like, 'Well, I didn't expect that when I asked, "What's your poison?"' will soon get the party back on track.

12

How to perform an emergency tracheotomy after pretending you're a surgeon

So far your ruse has worked. Your new girlfriend believes you're an eminent surgeon and she's suitably impressed. The responsibility... the kudos... the salary... the nimble and sensitive fingers... She's so into you as you stare into her eyes over a romantic candlelit dinner, regaling her with tales of the hundreds of lives you've saved. Then someone at another table starts choking.

It starts as an irritating cough but before long they sound like they're possessed. Someone performs the Heimlich manoeuvre but it doesn't work. 'Is there a doctor here?' someone screams in a faltering, panicked voice.

Then the inevitable cry from your partner, 'My boyfriend's an eminent surgeon!' and in moments you've gone from sitting to one side of the restaurant to being the centre of attention.

Remember the adage,
'It's better to try and
fail than not try at all'.

You have two choices:

1. Lose face by admitting you're really just a photocopier repairman from Swindon.
2. Confidently go along with the charade. As the adage goes, it's better to try and fail than not try at all.

(*Note*: someone might lose his/her life, but at least you saved face.)

TRACHEOTOMY FAQS

Is this a dangerous procedure that should really only be performed by a medical professional?
Yes.

Oh… What will I need?
A sharp knife; the hollow barrel of a biro or a drinking straw; balls.

What's next?
Find the cricothyroid membrane on the victim's neck.

The crico-what?
The cricothyroid membrane. The cricoid is the soft, smaller bump on the throat below the Adam's apple. That's where the incision will be made.

Incision? WTF! No one told me I had to cut stuff.
You're pretending to be a surgeon, idiot! It's what they do.

OK, then what?
Make a half-inch horizontal cut about a half-inch deep. Just below your cut you'll see the cricothyroid membrane. Make an incision on the membrane itself deep enough to gain access to the airway.

I feel faint...
Grow some.

Now what?
Insert the straw or biro tube about 5 centimetres (2 inches) into the windpipe. The victim should begin breathing on his/her own.

You said 'should'...
If you attempt the procedure and the person lives*, you'll be a hero.
If you do it wrong and he/she dies**, you'll still be that brave surgeon who failed doing the job he loved.
It's a win–win situation.

* unlikely
** almost inevitable

Note: If the victim dies and your girlfriend suspects that you may not actually be a surgeon, admit it. Say you're really a secret agent who had to pretend he was a surgeon.

13

The art of writing
a ransom note

Ransom notes can be one of the most profitable forms of writing in the world, second only to being Stieg Larsson, Dan Brown or J.K. Rowling. However, be aware that there are many pitfalls for the novice kidnapper, including the underuse of adjectives, rambling prose and sloppy punctuation.

Kidnappers the world over are unanimous in what makes an effective ransom note: you must make sure it's clear and concise. That way your recipient will be left in no doubt over the nature of the abduction and your demands.

STRUCTURE
An effective ransom note always contains the following 6 elements:

a. The victim's identity
b. Your ransom demand
c. The deadline

d. The threat

e. Logistics of the ransom payment; how the exchange of (a) for (b) will take place

f. Proof of life

Note: Omitting one or more of these elements (especially a, b or d) will severely compromise the effectiveness of your kidnapping.

FORMAT

Successful ransom notes tend to follow the following convention:

> *I have [a]. To ensure his/her safe return you must supply me with [b] by [c]. If these demands are not met I will [d]. To pay the ransom follow these instructions: [e].*
> *As proof that [a] is safe and well I enclose [f].*
> *Yours sincerely etc.,*

SOME DOS AND DON'TS WHEN WRITING RANSOM NOTES

- DO use a writing medium that places doubt on your mental state and which therefore implies a greater threat level. For example, crayons, letters cut from a newspaper, blood, excrement, someone else's excrement.
- DO make sure your note is written clearly. For example, a carelessly written number 7 can sometimes be confused with a 1, resulting in a ransom one-seventh of that expected.
- DON'T write the ransom note on your personal headed stationery (that's just asking for trouble).
- DO keep it simple. Sonnets, ballads and limericks are time-consuming and an unnecessary diversion.

- DO ensure the threat is menacing and ominous, and choose your adjectives accordingly. For example, death or maiming must always be 'prolonged' or 'grisly', never 'quick' or 'painless'.
- DON'T send an anonymous-looking severed finger, toe, ear or nose to the ransom payer. Unless the body part has a distinguishing feature like a birthmark, scar or tattoo, it will just represent savage butchery rather than actual proof of life.
- DON'T make demands that are unrealistic and impractical. For example, it's reasonable to ask a large multinational corporation to pay £1 million for the release of their CEO, but demanding the same sum for the return of your neighbour's cat is unlikely to result in anything other than the blood of a dead tabby on your hands.
- DON'T ask for the ransom to be paid in bitcoins, however fashionable this might seem. Cash is always far better than a peer-to-peer digital online currency.
- DON'T physically write the letter yourself; not even while wearing latex gloves. DNA is your enemy. If possible, force your victim to pen the letter, although this can cause logistical problems if your victim is illiterate, a baby or a pet.
- DO be careful with punctuation. A wrongly placed comma, full stop, colon or semi-colon can lead to misunderstandings, sometimes with comic (but more often, tragic) results.
- DO remember this phrase: 'Unmarked, non-sequential bills, high denominations only.'

14

Being best man at a shotgun wedding

Being a best man at a shotgun wedding is similar to being one at an ordinary wedding, the main difference being the groom will be getting married against his will. Understanding that there are certain differences to the best man's duties is essential to avoid both embarrassment *and* having the groom's death on your conscience.

If you're in doubt as to whether you will be officiating at a shotgun wedding, take this simple test:

HOW TO TELL IF YOU'RE THE BEST MAN AT AN ORDINARY WEDDING OR A SHOTGUN WEDDING

1. What is the main reason the couple are getting married?
a) So they can share their life and their love forever
b) Unplanned pregnancy

2. What is the main reason for the groom's pre-wedding nerves?
a) Commitment
b) Gunshot wounds or death

3. What are the names of the bridesmaids?
a) Polly, Sophie, Jess and Vicky
b) Daisy-Sue, Tammy-Mae, Mary-Belle and Patty-Lou

4. What is the main concern of the bride's father?
a) Will my future son-in-law be a good and loyal husband?
b) Will the gun jam?

Results

If you selected mainly bs then you're likely to be at a shotgun wedding. If this is the case, ensure you heed the advice that follows.

THE BEST MAN'S DUTIES AT A SHOTGUN WEDDING

Helping the groom select his suit

Depending on the time of day and the formality of the ceremony this could be a morning suit, a lounge suit, a tailcoat or a tuxedo. Wearing a Kevlar vest as an undergarment is considered unsporting and bad manners. If the bride's father spots this he is likely to attempt a head or neck shot, causing unwanted attention and a possible blood splatter all over the maid of honour.

Holding the wedding ring safely

It's your job to keep the ring safe and to present it at the appropriate time during the ceremony. This is one duty you absolutely do not want to screw up since the implications will be serious. If your ineptitude results in the inability of the wedding to proceed you're likely to end up on a mortician's slab rather than as a funny clip on *You've Been Framed*.

Your speech

The best man's speech is probably the task that causes the most anxiety – apart, of course, from the sight of a loaded gun trained on the groom, who is standing right next to you. The same guidelines that apply to a regular wedding apply here: the speech should thank the bride's parents by name, thank the guests for attending, and include some humorous/sentimental anecdotes about the groom.

<u>Ensure, however, you avoid these controversial topics</u>:
• pre–marital sex
• the age of consent
• pregnancy
• guns and anything related to firearms

Ensuring the band has the correct music for the first dance

Irrespective of the groom's wishes, use your discretion when it comes to the music. The father of the bride at a shotgun wedding tends not to possess a great sense of humour. The following songs are therefore more likely to be seen as an incitement to shoot than a light-hearted example of irony.

• 'Hit Me With Your Best Shot' by Pat Benatar
• 'Sweating Bullets' by Megadeth
• 'Shot Through The Heart' by Bon Jovi
• 'Man Down' by Rihanna
• 'Eton Rifles' by The Jam

- 'One Shot' by JLS
- 'Bang Bang' by will.i.am
- 'Shots Fired' by Slash
- Anything by Guns N' Roses

CRUCIAL ADVICE

And as tempting as it may seem, do not, under any circumstances, use this line at any point in the ceremony to get a laugh:

'It was a matter of wife or death.'

15

Removing an archbishop's blood from a hotel carpet

Theological arguments with the senior clergy can often get out of hand. One moment you're in a hotel bar with an archbishop involved in a highly animated and passionate debate about predestination versus free will. Tempers and voices get raised so you decide to take the argument back to your room. Things escalate when you're discussing Calvinism and, in the heat of the moment, you hit the archbishop around the head with a heavy table lamp and he's lying stone-dead on the floor.

If this is the case, your first action must be to remove any evidence of the crime.

The most important advice is: **Don't panic! With patience and diligence, you can remove any trace of the blood.**

Note: It's important to deal with the stain as soon as possible… dried or congealed archbishop blood is far harder to remove.

With diligence and care, even the most stubborn archbishop's bloodstain can be removed from a hotel carpet.

BEFORE YOU START
• Put the 'Do Not Disturb' sign on the door and lock it.
• Hide the body for later disposal.

THE PROCESS
1. Soak a clean absorbent towel in cold water and use this to carefully blot the bloodstain.
2. Dissolve 1kg (2lb) of table salt in a gallon of cool water. Using the same towel, dab the archbishop bloodstain with the solution until it is completely diluted.
3. Gently wash the area of the stain with a mixture of lukewarm water and a mild household (non-bleach) detergent.
4. Blot the whole area with a clean absorbent towel.
5. Leave to air dry.

Warning
• Do not attempt to accelerate the process by using a hair dryer. This can cause the stain to set.
• Never scrub archbishop bloodstains; this tends to make them worse.
• Household ammonia (or hair bleach in an emergency) can remove archbishop blood more quickly; however, this can stain or damage the carpet and the telltale smell can alert hotel staff.

If you are in a hurry
Rather than cleaning it, consider moving a heavy piece of furniture over the bloodstain.
SEE ALSO: Disposing of a dead body (p.85).

16

Shouting out the wrong name in a moment of passion

It's a medical fact that in the heat of passion, blood is diverted from your brain to other extremities with the result that your mental faculties can become impaired. This could result in you forgetting easy capital cities or collective nouns; however, the most common and awkward consequence is the calling of your partner by a different name.

In the best-case scenario the name you yell out will be a completely random one with absolutely no relevance to either party – but this will never happen. The reality is that it will inevitably be that of an ex, your partner's best friend or, more worryingly, your sibling.

If your partner hears you addressing them by the wrong name once you can usually get away with it just by denial. Chances are they'll be convinced that such was the intensity of the experience – or their own insecurities – that they imagined it.

If you call them by the wrong name more than once, however, then a range of excuses is needed to salvage the situation. Whatever of the following methods you choose there are two key requirements for damage limitation: *be quick and be confident.*

TWO SUREFIRE WAYS TO AVOID SHOUTING OUT THE WRONG NAME

- Make sure every one of your partners has the exact same name.

- Only date people called 'Slow down!', 'Oh God!', 'Yes! Yes! Yes! Yes! Yessssssss!' or 'Move your leg'.

THE BEST EXCUSES

The celebrity comparison

This is easy – as soon as the last syllable of the name leaves your mouth instantly add the surname of an attractive, sexy celebrity, plus the phrase: '*That's* who you remind me of!' For example, 'George' becomes 'George Clooney' and 'Megan' might be 'Megan Fox'.

Note: Resist the temptation to turn 'Steve' into 'Steve Buscemi' or 'Camilla' into 'Camilla Parker-Bowles'. Such comparisons will neither impress nor convince your partner.

Blame an evil presence

After shouting the name immediately add the phrase: '*Begone foul spirit!*' Explain that you felt an evil presence in the bedroom and the random name you just shouted out was your ex, who killed him/herself after you broke up, and who has now returned to pester you.

Blame a benign presence

After shouting the name immediately add, '*Thank you for your blessing!*' Explain that you felt the spirit of your late grandmother/grandfather in the bedroom and shouted out his/her name. Tell your partner that he/she told you they approve of the relationship and send their best wishes.

Cause a distraction

Immediately after shouting out the wrong name cause a diversion. Throw the nearest heavy object against a window, for example, and shout 'My God, someone's trying to break in!' By the time you've searched the house/the police have left the premises, your partner will have forgotten all about your indiscretion and will be too frightened to get amorous again, saving you from any further embarrassment that evening.

Pretend to faint

As soon as the last syllable of the wrong name leaves your mouth keel over and collapse to the floor. Fake unconsciousness for as long as you can comfortably pull it off without smirking or laughing. When you open your eyes say, 'Where am I... What happened... When did you get here?' Your partner will be so shocked that he/she will either completely forget your name blunder, or if he/she does remember, will put it down to the embolism or mini-stroke responsible for your collapse.

Syllable modification

As soon as you hear the first syllable of the wrong name leaving your mouth use it to start a whole new word... preferably one with relevance to your partner or your situation. For example, if you were about to yell, 'Antonia' or 'Anthony', stop yourself after 'Ant...' and start a sentence:

Good examples
• 'Anticipation. My heart almost explodes when I think of you in my arms once more.'
• 'Antidote. I hope I never find one for your love.'

Bad examples
• 'Anteater. That's what your nose reminds me of.'
• 'Antibiotics. That's the only thing that will clear my chlamydia.'

Invent an acronym
You need to think fast on your feet (or back) in order to pull this off. For example, if you shout out 'Fran', say it stands for 'Faithful, Romantic, Amorous & Nice'. Likewise, 'Pete' would represent 'Passionate, Exciting, Tender, Eye-candy'.
Note: You're probably better off trying out a different excuse if the name you shout out in error is Chandraprakash or Brzenczyszczykiewicz.

Claim it's the name of a fancy restaurant (this excuse works best when a male name is called out)
Immediately add an 's' to the name and explain that you've been racking your brain trying to remember the place where you want to take your partner for a truly romantic dinner... and you suddenly thought of it. Fancy restaurants are usually named after their famous chef, so a European-sounding name is most convincing: Carlo's, Marco's, Pierre's or Franco's.
Note: Not many leading chefs are called Billy-Joe, Duane or Barry.

Claim it's your pet name for your sexual organs
It's far preferable to freak your partner out (or at least disturb them a lot) than admit the truth. In this crazy, mixed-up world who's to say whether calling your penis 'Angela' or your vagina 'David' is right or wrong? And what's 'normal' anyway?

Note: If all else fails, just admit your mistake and say, 'Get over it.'

17

Evacuating a sinking ship: Is it really 'Women and children first'?

As your luxury cruise liner lists at 20 degrees two things will usually go through your mind: The first is the empty promises peddled by the cruise operators of 'an all-inclusive romantic holiday of a lifetime; a great chance to meet people and visit multiple destinations with the benefit of only having to unpack once'.

The second is whether the traditional code of conduct of 'Women and children first' must be adhered to. The good news for men is that there is absolutely no legal basis for the protocol of 'Women and children first' in international maritime law – and consequently, no need to dress as a woman or child in order to ensure your safety.

The code, which was popularised during the sinking of RMS *Titanic*, has its origins in the ideals of Edwardian chivalry and, as such, is as irrelevant today as most examples of Edwardian etiquette, such as not smoking in the presence of a lady or commencing a conversation with an allusion to the weather.

FOUR REASONS YOU KNOW IT'S TIME TO GRAB YOUR LIFE JACKET AND ABANDON SHIP

1. You hear the General Emergency Alarm consisting of 7 short blasts followed by 1 long blast of the ship's horn or whistle.
2. You see an ashen-faced Italian captain and crew barge past you with expressions that are at once both anxious and guilty.
3. Your fellow passengers/loved-ones are sliding rather than walking.
4. Your feet are wet and you're not in one of the following: the bath, shower, swimming pool or Jacuzzi.

THE ADVANTAGES OF IGNORING THE CODE OF CONDUCT OUTWEIGH ANY DISADVANTAGES

Disadvantages
You'll probably be branded a coward and nicknamed 'yellow belly', 'chicken', 'wuss' or 'sissy'.

Advantages
You won't go to an icy, watery grave.

Conclusion
Forget 'women and children first'. In times of disaster, it's every man for himself!
Note: If you're female the bad news is that you have no automatic right to safe evacuation. The good news, however, is that men

who ignore the protocol are actually supporting feminists who view the code as an example of benevolent sexism and unwarranted male privilege.

18

Delivering bad medical news by ventriloquism

Despite critics calling it 'the pinnacle of tactlessness' and 'the notion of an insensitive lunatic', the principle of doctors and consultants using a ventriloquist's doll to deliver bad news to a patient or his/her family is growing in popularity among the medical profession.

Supporters point to the fact that this method can often soften the blow when a patient hears the stark news that he/she is suffering from a dangerous disease or terminal condition. Additionally, from the doctor's point of view, having a third party (albeit a wood and fabric doll) make the diagnosis helps limit any emotional trauma he/she might suffer themselves.

If you are going to deliver results by ventriloquism it's essential that you follow these established guidelines in order to ensure a) your patient is relaxed, and b) you're able to convey the news as clearly as possible.

IMPORTANT

The following guidelines assume you are reasonably proficient in ventriloquism. Nothing undermines your authority more than telling a patient they are suffering from 'colio' or 'smallcox'.

PUT YOUR PATIENT AT EASE RIGHT AWAY

Your patient will already be suffering from high anxiety in advance of getting his/her diagnosis. Add to this the sight of a creepy-looking doll sitting on your knee or at the edge of a hospital bed and you can understand that it's absolutely essential that you immediately put them at ease.

Good ventriloquist dolls to use

Those dressed as medical professionals (doctors, nurses, consultants, clinical technicians) help convey the appropriate degree of authority and gravitas.

Bad ventriloquist dolls to use

Those that are frightening or resemble animals; no one wants to hear Chucky tell them they have lymphoma. Equally, no one will believe a monkey proclaiming they have only 6 months to live.

AVOID CONDITIONS THAT INCLUDE THE LETTERS B, F, M, P, Q, V AND W

While those with even basic ventriloquism skills can say 'cancer', 'coma', 'syphilis' or even 'heart disease' without moving their lips, only the very best ventriloquists can master what are known as the '7 troublesome letters'.

Without the necessary skills, ebola will usually come out as 'egola' and herpes will be 'herkeys'. At best this leads to comic confusion but in practice it often ends in tragic misunderstanding and a false sense of optimism from the patient. Know your limitations!

> **Only skilled ventriloquists should attempt any of the following:**
> • Alzheimer's
> • Dementia
> • Diabetes
> • Hepatitis
> • Malaria
> • Multiple sclerosis
> • Polio
> • Anything involving the word 'brain'

HAVE SOME GOOD COMEBACKS FOR HECKLERS

Even ventriloquists are not immune to unwanted interruptions from their audience (i.e. the patient). Nothing will put you off your routine or dent your confidence than someone heckling you while you try to deliver the bad news. Have a stock of well-rehearsed and proven comebacks, for example:

• 'Why don't you stand in that corner and finish evolving?'
• 'Your bus leaves in 10 minutes... be under it.'
• 'Yeah, well I'm not the one with leukaemia.'

19

Accidentally wearing a Nazi uniform to your niece's wedding

Dress codes can be very confusing and also open to interpretation, which is why turning up at a place of worship or a registry office looking like a prominent member of the SS or Gestapo is a more common occurrence than you might imagine.

Getting disapproving glances as you shuffle along to your seat wearing the dress uniform of a Waffen-SS Obergruppenführer complete with death's head badge and oak leaf insignia can be awkward; however, the situation is usually salvageable, and red faces often avoided, by following one simple piece of advice: **style it out.**

Look your hosts, the bride and groom, other guests and the clergy straight in the eye and shamelessly offer one of the following excuses:

• 'Sorry, I've come straight from work.'(*Note*: There is no need to elaborate here.)

Misinterpreting dress codes for social occasions is more common than you might imagine.

- 'I thought it was a themed wedding: *Inglourious Basterds*.'
- Point to the bride and say, 'You know she's related by marriage to Hermann Goering.'
- 'This? It's what all the fashionistas are wearing this season.'
- 'My psychiatrist said I have delusions of grandeur.'
- 'Didn't (bride's name) tell you I was an actor? I've just done some re-shoots on a comedy remake of *Schindler's List*.'
- 'Well, *I* call it smart casual.'

20

Organising a vigilante gang

L eading a vast citizen's army through dark, rain-drenched
streets armed with baseball bats and claw hammers,
hunting down and inflicting summary justice on criminals and
ne'er-do-wells (or those you think are criminals and ne'er-do-
wells). What's not to like?

While this scenario and the whole concept of 'frontier justice'
certainly has its appeal, organising a vigilante gang is nowhere
near as easy as it sounds and considerable time and thought
must go into the following: recruiting gang members, choosing
your name, your uniform and your walk.

RECRUITING GANG MEMBERS

Number of members
In simple terms it's more than 3 and less than 20. If your vigilante
gang consists of just 3 people you'll simply become known as
'those 3 troublemakers' or 'Bob and his 2 friends'. More than
20 and the gang becomes too large to control and is likely to

split into different factions, leading to in-fighting, leadership challenges and your probable expulsion. Or beating.

Type of members
You should recruit only members who demonstrate the following character traits:
• Disregard authority
• Blindly follow orders
• Ignore the consequences of their actions

GANG NAMES
These should be cool, imply strength and menace – and, for credibility, be relevant. For example, don't use the prefix '18th Street' if you actually live on Acacia Avenue; likewise, avoid calling yourselves the Latino Army if you're not Latino and there's only 3 of you.

Good gang names	Bad gang names
North Side Posse	The 10th-Street Stamp Collectors
South Side Assassins	The Cupcake Crew
18th-Street Brotherhood	The Moderately Angry
The Bounty Hunters	The Pansies
Los Villainos	The Librarians
East Side Bloods	The Friendly Pals
The Hammerlords	The Chess Club
Iron Horsemen	The Skipping Boyz
Murder Squad	Timmy Mallet's Army
The Devil's Disciples	The Proficient Readers
Four Corner Cobras	The Anorexic Paedos
Red Hand Syndicate	Mr Potato Head
Soldiers of Retribution	The Rainbow Gaylords

UNIFORMS

Vigilante gangs need to wear some sort of uniform in order to recognise each other and also to look tough. Trying to get gang members to agree to wear the same outfit is often challenging. Black suits some but not others and not everyone can carry off a beret. At the time of writing Gok Wan hadn't made a TV show called *Gang Fashion Fix*, so be prepared to experiment, improvise and mix and match to achieve a look that says 'I'm threatening yet responsible'.

Good things to wear
- Dark colours so you can become 'at one with the night'
- Leather jackets
- Plain T-shirts (resist the temptation to have the name of your gang emblazoned on it as this is considered tacky)
- Combat trousers
- Bandanas
- Berets
- Biker boots
- Sunglasses

Bad things to wear
- Floral prints
- Christmas sweaters
- High-vis jackets
- Anything made of suede or lambswool
- Tutus
- Leg warmers
- Anything that makes it look as if you're in an advert for an online dating service
- Uggs

THE WALK

It's important that you adopt a tough, stylised walk. For example, take long, determined strides with your chest puffed out slightly. Avoid hopping and skipping since this will undermine any sense of threat. Also, avoid walking backwards; while unique, this is just stupid.

21

Suspecting your girlfriend is a serial killer

Whether it's her number of former partners, her previous job as a cage dancer, her weight or that secret obsession with Duncan from Blue, women like to keep secrets. In most cases these are relatively innocuous deceptions that don't harm a relationship. However, sometimes the web of deceit is wide and sticky. One of the most heinous acts of duplicity is when she leads a double life as a serial killer.

Many men feel awkward confronting a partner with their suspicions and to be frank, it's pointless anyway. If she ISN'T a serial killer, she'll be incredibly upset and angry that you ever suspected she was; if she IS a serial killer, she'll deny it anyway, then murder you in your sleep since you know too much.

Rather than challenging her right away, instead complete this simple 10-question survey that will help you assess the likelihood and determine your next course of action.

Step 1

CONSIDER THE SIGNS

1. Does she buy Stain Devils for blood removal in bulk?
   ☐ Yes ☐ No
2. Is she always looking through the phone book, writing down names and addresses completely at random?
   ☐ Yes ☐ No
3. Has she recently changed her name by deed poll to Hannibal? ☐ Yes ☐ No
4. Does she leave the flat every night at 11pm with an axe and come back in the early hours, saying she's 'just been for a breath of fresh air'? ☐ Yes ☐ No
5. Does she gaze longingly at the skinned carcasses hanging in the butcher's window, even though she's a strict lacto-vegetarian? ☐ Yes ☐ No
6. Is she always receiving brochures from surgical supply companies in the post? ☐ Yes ☐ No
7. Have you ever discovered that your Black & Decker circular saw is covered in what she claims is just 'red paint'?
   ☐ Yes ☐ No
8. Does her new scarf looks suspiciously like a small intestine?
   ☐ Yes ☐ No
9. Is there a naked leg sticking out from under her side of the bed? ☐ Yes ☐ No
10. Is her email address psychokiller114@hotmail.co.uk?
    ☐ Yes ☐ No

Step 2

TAKE THE APPROPRIATE ACTION

If you answered 'Yes' to 1–4 questions:
The evidence is coincidental or at best circumstantial. There is no need to adjust your behaviour.

If you answered 'Yes' to 5–7 questions:
Some cause for concern. Play safe and dump her. Useful lines are 'It's not you, it's me', 'I'm not ready to commit' or 'I'm in fear of my life'.

If you answered 'Yes' to 8–10 questions:
For the love of God, run!

22

Chatting someone up at a funeral

While the primary purpose of a funeral is to celebrate, remember and consecrate the life of someone recently deceased, a welcome consequence of the event is that it offers an excellent opportunity to meet a wide variety of people of the opposite sex. Your presence means you already have something in common with them: the departed.

The nature of a funeral means that the mourners (particularly if they are close friends or family) will be in a very vulnerable, emotional state. As a result, they are more likely to be pre-disposed towards receiving compliments and possibly even date propositions.

CHAT-UP/ICE-BREAKER LINES
These should be comforting, considered and reflective, not cheap, crude and insensitive.

Think Mr Darcy from *Pride and Prejudice*, not Joey from *Friends*...

The good thing about meeting someone at a funeral is that you already have something in common: the departed.

GOOD: 'Your tears are like shining crystals of pure sadness; the salted waters of a broken heart.'
BAD: 'You look really hot in black.'

GOOD: 'What the heart has once known, it shall never forget.'
BAD: 'Cheer up, no one's died.'

GOOD: 'Death leaves a heartache no one can heal; love leaves a memory no one can steal.'
BAD: 'He's gone to a better place... Do you want to come back to mine?'

GOOD: 'Shared grief is half the sorrow, but happiness when shared, is doubled.'
BAD: 'I hear he donated his organs... Well, I've got one you might like.'

GOOD: 'Death is the last chapter in time, but the first chapter in eternity.'
BAD: 'How do you fancy putting the "fun" back in "funeral"?'

GOOD: 'To live in the hearts of those we love is never to die.'
BAD: 'You, me, whipped cream and handcuffs... Any questions?'

GOOD: 'Sorrow is a fruit; God does not allow it to grow on a branch that is too weak to bear it.'
BAD: 'How YOU doin'?'

Improving your chances with women
Deliver the line while gently wiping away their mascara that has run.

Improving your chances with Goths
As above.

Business cards
It is acceptable to hand out business cards containing your personal contact details provided these have a thin black border.

Special advice if you're trying to chat-up the partner of the departed
Avoid this line: 'So I guess it means you're not seeing anyone...'

23

Being asked to join a witches' coven

Forget book clubs, film societies or amateur dramatics... if you want to belong to an exciting social group a coven wins hands down. This gathering of witches (usually 13) is a great way to meet like-minded individuals, run around woodland at midnight and see members of the opposite sex naked. How often does that happen playing bridge?

Due to the inherent secrecy surrounding the practice of witchcraft, any approach to recruit you to a coven is likely to be discrete. Unless you're already a white witch, being asked to join a coven will naturally come as a surprise and the first question you'll be asking is: 'Why me?' Usually there are two reasons: the person asking will have observed you for a while and recognised that you possess innate witchy powers – or it's just a flimsy excuse to see you naked under a full moon.

FIFTEEN REASONS WHY SOMEONE MIGHT THINK YOU MIGHT HAVE SPIRITUAL OR MAGICAL POWERS:

1. Your Facebook identity is Woodsprite or Moondaughter.
2. You spend far too much time hanging around New Age shops, fondling crystals and chatting about chalices and faeries.
3. Your tramp stamp is a pentangle.
4. You have a cat called Salem, Pyewocket or Crookshanks.
5. You prefer the Vernal Equinox to Christmas.
6. You pooh-pooh vitamins or food supplements, instead claiming to 'get my energy from the Earth and the sky'.
7. Your bumper sticker reads: 'My other car is a broomstick'.
8. You own the complete box set of *Sabrina*.
9. You view Halloween as a religious holiday rather than an over-commercialised travesty.
10. You prefer to cook in a cauldron rather than a Le Creuset casserole dish.
11. When asked what you're currently reading you reply 'auras'.
12. There's an altar in your lounge.
13. You have a timeshare near Stonehenge.
14. You have a tattoo that says, 'We're all jewels in an infinitely connected web of silken joy'.
15. You look like Kate Bush when she was hot.

If you *are* asked to join a coven then you should be honoured. Witches are extremely cautious about who they ask for fear of revealing the secrets of the 'Craft' and the identities of other members. Only you can tell if you'll be comfortable in such a group; if you're not sure whether joining a coven is for you, consider the following:

COVEN FAQS

Can a man be a witch?
Yes, but like calling yourself a 'male nurse', everyone sniggers and doesn't really take you seriously.

I've heard that covens are composed of normal members of society…
That's not strictly true since most normal members of society don't want to undress and recite incantations and spells.

What is 'Magick'?
A pretentious way of spelling magic.

Black makes me look fat. Will that be an issue?
No, but stick to dark colours. Wearing pastels or DayGlo gymwear is not conducive to being at one with nature.

Will I be able to cast spells like Harry Potter?
No.

What about Hermione Granger then?
No.

Ron Weasley?
Stop it, you're an idiot!

TEN REASONS TO JOIN A COVEN

1. You legitimately get the chance to spell 'magic' with a 'k' at the end of it.
2. You can tell friends, relatives or co-workers that you're in a coven and therefore appear cool and super-spooky.
3. You can work your way up to become a high priest or priestess... a much more impressive job title than bought ledger clerk.
4. You get the opportunity to conjure up a spirit or two.
5. Casting spells is a great party piece.
6. Being called a pagan is really edgy.
7. You can learn to put a hex on that annoying neighbour.
8. It's more interesting than joining a Pilates class.
9. You can find like-minded individuals who won't think you're a nut job.
10. Ritual nudity.

24

Avoiding small talk with your hairdresser

Having your hair cut is supposed to be a relaxing and soothing experience, a chance to zone out and unwind while your scalp is gently massaged and all your cares and anxieties wash slowly away down the plughole. Unfortunately, any chance of entering this Zen-like state is usually curtailed by being asked inane questions about reality TV, holidays or Christmas shopping (which is likely to be a topic of conversation any time from 15 October to 24 December).

Either due to the fact that it makes them feel uncomfortable or because they fear it will result in some sort of bad haircut retribution, many people feel uneasy saying to their hairdresser, 'Sorry, I can't talk right now' or simply 'Shut the fuck up'. If you're one of those people, the following advice will help you enjoy a more peaceful time at the salon.

EIGHT WAYS TO CUT THE CONVERSATION WHILE HAVING YOUR HAIR CUT

One-word answers
Answering any question with a single word is guaranteed to frustrate your hairdresser and curtail any conversation. Words to use: 'Yes', 'No', 'Maybe' and 'Giraffe'.

Act creepy
When asked what you're doing tonight, look left and right, then whisper conspiratorially, 'I've got to clean up the blood and bury the body.'

Hobby time
Engross yourself in a pastime that involves so much of your attention and concentration that it's obvious that you don't have any time to engage in conversation. Good hobbies to practice while sat in the chair include reading, crochet, sudoku, quilting, scrimshaw, harmonica, origami, Tarot, juggling and masturbation.

Change the topic
It's easy to get your hairdresser out of his/her comfort zone... just divert the conversation from anything you'd find in *Heat* or *OK!* magazines and they'll start floundering. As soon as you can, begin talking about any one of the following:
• The spiritual teachings of Gurdjieff
• The Kyoto Protocol
• The death of socialism
• Open source software
• Keynesian economics
• Plato's 'Allegory of the Cave'
• Anything involving the words: 'Marx', 'caucus' or 'subatomic'

Pretend you have no voice box
Hold an electric shaver to your throat and in your best impersonation of Stephen Hawking say that years of heavy smoking have resulted in a laryngectomy. Your hairdresser will soon get fed up or freaked out by the sound of what appears to be a Dalek in the salon.

Religious reasons
Hand your hairdresser a piece of paper that says you've become a Carmelite Nun and have taken a vow of silence. Show another piece of paper that says any attempt to coerce you into conversation will be considered a religious hate crime.

Delaying tactic
After your hairdresser asks the first question say, 'Hmm, let me think about that.' Look into the middle distance and frown slightly. Remain this way throughout the appointment.

Pretend you have a stutter
Taking ninety seconds to answer the question, 'Did you watch the Kardashians on telly last night?' is certain to annoy any hairdresser into silence.

25

Disposing of a
dead body

Sometimes the death may be deliberate; other times it might be accidental but a bit awkward to explain. In either case, you'll have a body to dispose of and it's only a matter of time before someone gets suspicious and starts asking you questions beginning with the words 'Have you seen...?'

Disposing of a human body is harder than you might think. It's not like throwing your dog's poop over your neighbour's fence and hoping he doesn't realise. For a start, teeth and bones are notoriously difficult to destroy completely, while blood is both profuse and messy.

Scientific advances mean that any remains, however inconsequential, can provide damning forensic evidence; the key therefore to the successful disposal of a dead body is being thorough. What's more, a body will begin to smell three to six hours after death (sooner if it's unseasonably warm), which means you have to think and act fast. To avoid suspicion and eventual arrest, adopt one of the following methods.

*Burying a body at home
can sometimes attract
unwanted attention.*

BEFORE YOU START

Make sure you're well-prepared by ensuring you have the following:
- Tarpaulin
- Gloves
- Saw and selection of sharp knives
- Shovel
- Strong rope
- Stronger alibi

PROVEN DISPOSAL METHODS

Acid bath
Method: Dissolve the body by immersing it in concentrated sulphuric acid.
Pros: The body will be complete destroyed.
Cons: Have you ever tried to buy four barrels of concentrated sulphuric acid anywhere?

Quicklime
Method: Pour an amount of quicklime (calcium oxide) over the body and add water to start the decomposition. Repeat as necessary.
Pros: Good for a Victorian-themed body disposal.
Cons: Unless the proportion of quicklime and water is exact, the heat generated by the chemical reaction will just mummify the body, therefore preserving it... the complete opposite of what you had in mind.

Burial at home
Method: Dig a large hole. Insert body. Back fill and disguise the excavation.
Pros: No messy dismemberment.
Cons: Need to explain to spouse/neighbours why you've suddenly felt the urge to install an ornamental fountain/sunken Italian garden or re-lay the patio. On your own. At midnight.

Viking funeral
Method: Attach weights to the body and place it in a replica longboat. Douse in petrol, set it alight and push the boat out to sea.
Pros: Body is likely to be burned beyond recognition and even if parts remain, they'll sink to the seabed.
Cons: It's often quite difficult sourcing a replica Viking long-boat – and if you're not of Norse decent, it's sometimes difficult to explain why you've suddenly got an interest in sending the spirits of a loved one to the mighty halls of Valhalla.

Feed it to the pigs
Method: The title says it all.
Pros: Pigs will eat anything, including teeth and bones.
Cons: Dragging a body to your local petting zoo is likely to attract unwanted attention.

Improvised cremation
Method: Cover the body with old leaves and branches and set fire to it, like a bonfire.
Pros: Intense heat can reduce a body to about 3kg (6lb) of ash in about 3 hours and there's no accurate way to test for DNA.
Cons: To completely destroy the body you'll need a temperature

of about 871 degrees Celsius (1,600 degrees Fahrenheit); to put this in perspective, it's about the same temperature as a jet engine exhaust... Difficult to achieve with just a can of petrol and a barbecue fire starter.

Dumping the body in woodland
Method: Take the body into nearby woods. Come back without it.
Pros: It's easy.
Cons: Someone will find the body; they always do.

Sliced 'n diced
Method: Chop the body into as many small pieces as possible, then dispose of these in weighted sacks in multiple rivers.
Pros: It worked on *The Sopranos*.
Cons: Cutting up the body... bagging the parts... cleaning up the blood... finding enough rocks... and sacks... driving all over the country to dispose of them... Too much hard work.

Recycling
Method: Dismember body, mince it into small pieces and use the contents in pies.
Pros: Virtually impossible to trace the body.
Cons: Need to write a detailed business plan for a pie shop and secure a bank loan to finance it, then locate suitable premises with a short-term lease and invest in shop fitting and marketing. Or enter into protracted discussions with Greggs to persuade them to take 4,000 pies that taste like body parts.

Tibetan sky burial

Method: Despite its name, this method proves that Tibetans don't really get the concept of burial. This Vajrayana Buddhist tradition involves leaving the corpse on a mountaintop where it will eventually be eaten by birds or decomposed by the elements.

Pros: Nature does the work for you.

Cons: Not recommended if you need to dispose of the body in a hurry. Handy mountaintops are usually quite difficult to find. As are vultures.

Freeze Drying (also known as Promession)

Method: The body is frozen so it becomes brittle; vibration then causes it to shatter into small pieces which are then turned into a fine powder.

Pros: The kudos of being involved in truly cutting edge corpse disposal.

Cons: This method assumes you have ready access to a large vat of liquid nitrogen.

26

Turning down an invitation to speak at a social event

According to psychologists, public speaking is our number one fear; more people are scared of standing in front of an audience than even death, heights, loneliness or being trapped in a lift with Justin Bieber. Although most of us realise that public speaking is a completely irrational fear, unlikely to result in any real or lasting harm, just the thought of having to address a room full of people, especially strangers, is enough to result in anxiety or panic attacks days or even weeks before the occasion itself.

Declining the invitation with an outright 'No' can be considered rude and discourteous, so it's best to say you have some sort of condition or intention that makes the host feel uneasy and likely to withdraw the invitation themself.

TEN SURE-FIRE EXCUSES TO PREVENT PEOPLE ASKING YOU TO SPEAK IN PUBLIC

Excuse 1: You've become a member of the South African Xhosa tribe
It's rare for any speech that is delivered with a series of vocal clicks to have sustained dramatic effect.

Excuse 2: Your speeches always follow a Quentin Tarantino-type narrative
Tell your host you eschew the conventional linear structure and instead your after-dinner speech will start at the end and then move to the beginning, then on to the middle, involving several arbitrary flashbacks to seemingly unconnected previous events.

Excuse 3: You only feel comfortable delivering a speech in mime
No matter how expressive your face or how flappy your hands are, a wedding toast performed entirely in mime will nearly always lack emotional impact.

Excuse 4: You have Tourette's
Many elderly guests could be upset when your grace before meals involves the words 'arsehole', 'bollocks' and 'shitty-shit-shit-shit'.

Excuse 5: You intend to use the speech to make a political point
The sincerity of a toast at a 25th wedding anniversary will be undermined when you turn your speech into a rant about climate change, genetically modified fruit or the Australian government's treatment of the Aborigines.

Excuse 6: You have an astonishing stutter
This will prevent you from adhering to the fundamental advice for any public speaker: keep it short.

Excuse 7: You only feel comfortable delivering a speech in limerick form
This might sound bizarre – unbelievable even – but the rhythm and meter of poetry can help many public speakers relax. However, your host might feel uncomfortable when he/she learns that your sensitive and poignant eulogy for their dear friend begins, 'A corpse that's rotting and smelly...'

Excuse 8: You're possessed
No one wants to have a series of heart-warming tributes at a retirement dinner interrupted by you rolling your eyes back in their sockets and saying in a hoarse, guttural voice that you hope your colleague 'rots and lies stinking in the Earth' – before projectile vomiting over the buffet table.

Excuse 9: You want to deliver your speech as a palindrome
It's rare to have the opportunity to stand up, clear your throat, look around a room full of captains of industry and announce: 'An igloo costs a lot, Ed! Amen. One made to last! So cool, Gina!'

Excuse 10: You're a stand-up comedian and you want to use the event to try out some new material
Your host and guests might be upset when they hear these sorts of lines in a best man's speech:

'I'm not saying the bride's fat but she was born with a silver shovel in her mouth.'

'And have you seen the mother-in-law? She's so ugly they use her in prisons to cure sex offenders.'

'And that maid of honour? She only wears knickers to keep her ankles warm.'

'You know the bride's mother lies about her age. I found out she used to babysit Yoda.'

'The bride's family have no class. I went to their house and asked to use the bathroom. They said, "Pick a corner"'

'And the bride's kid brother? I'm not saying he's a slime ball but he's listed as an ingredient in Mazola.'

'So what do you give a paedophile priest who has everything? A bigger parish.'

'Have you met the chief bridesmaid? She's a carpenter's dream: flat as a board and easy to nail.'

27

Being invited to an Amish party

Childish drinking contests, jumping in swimming pools fully clothed, snogging under the coats… all these things are noticeable by their absence at an Amish party… as too is any form of recorded music, alcohol, dancing or selfies.

On the face of it, there aren't that many reasons to go to an Amish party unless you're Amish, but sometimes when you receive a neatly inscribed card that says, 'You are cordially invited to celebrate the raising of our new barn', it's difficult to turn it down.

Many people are nervous and unsure about what to expect. Relax. Just follow the advice below and you'll have an enjoyable time at the party. Remember, the Amish are just like you and me (that is, if we shunned electricity and fun).

GOOD CONVERSATION OPENERS FOR AMISH PARTIES

- 'Thomas Edison, eh? What a troublemaker!'
- 'Saw your new buggy parked outside. Pretty trick!'
- 'So these must be your ten children…'
- 'Nice bonnet!'
- 'Those Mennonites, eh? What a bunch of namby-pamby liberals!'
- 'I don't think I could pull off that shade of black.'
- 'Photography? Yeah… it's so overrated.'
- 'So… know any good cheese-making stories?'
- 'Those quilts are hand-made? No way!'
- 'Hey, aren't you friends with Jebediah?'
- 'I just love what you've done with this barn!'

And when the chance comes to chat someone up…

GOOD PICK-UP LINES TO USE AT AMISH PARTIES

- 'I've got a thing for beards.'
- 'That apron really brings out your eyes.'
- 'Know why I believe in God? Because you're the answer to all my prayers.'
- 'You look really fit. Do a lot of ploughing?'
- 'I wish you had electricity because then I could really turn you on.'
- 'You look just like Harrison Ford/Kelly McGillis.'
- 'Hey baby, I put the "stud" into bible study.'
- 'Now I know why Solomon had 700 wives… he never met you.'
- 'I never knew angels flew this low.'

- 'If you never sin then how come you've just stolen my heart?'
- 'Hi, I'm Will. As in "God's Will." *
- 'The bible says, "Give drink to those who are thirsty, and feed the hungry"... How about dinner?'
- 'I'd really like to get to know you... and when I say "know", it's in the biblical sense.'
- 'When I look at you I think of Genesis chapter 3; my serpent wants to enter your garden.'
- 'What are you doing for the rest of your Afterlife?'
- 'It's like we belong with Noah... we make a perfect pair.'

* To pull this off your name should ideally be Will.

A BAD PICK-UP LINE TO USE AT AMISH PARTIES

'I was reading the Book of Numbers and then realised I don't have yours.'
(Since the Amish do not have telephones in their homes this pick-up line is pointless.)

28

Concealing an office affair from co-workers

Given the amount of time we spend at work, it's not at all surprising that many people end up having a romantic liaison with a colleague. But it's not the remit of this book to condone or criticise this behaviour, just to offer advice. In this case the advice is how to keep it a secret from nosey, prying co-workers who rely on the following to get them through the day: caffeine-laced drinks, energy bars and copious amounts of gossip.

Nothing says 'I'm having an office affair' better than coming back from the lunch break with your blouse inside out or ending internal phone calls with 'No, *you* hang up first!' Follow these recommendations to keep your relationship discrete.

TWELVE WAYS TO KEEP YOUR OFFICE ROMANCE A SECRET

1. Head off the gossip
Inevitable as the A4 paper running out halfway through printing

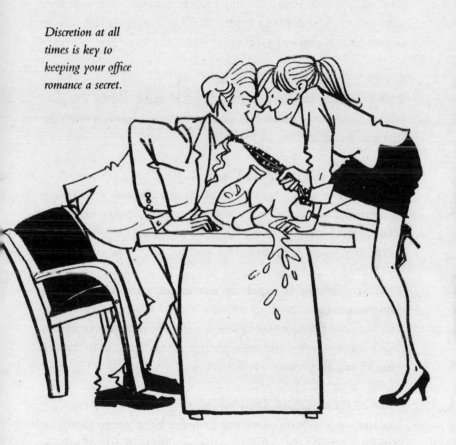

Discretion at all times is key to keeping your office romance a secret.

a large report, someone will get suspicious and rumours will start. The best way to take the heat off your relationship is to start spreading gossip of your own... but make sure it's so incredibly salacious that it becomes the number one topic du jour. Ideally this gossip should involve a senior staff member and one of the following topics: fraud, self-harm, black magic or gender realignment surgery.

2. Don't leave physical evidence
This could be anything from a lipstick mark, a pair of split-crotch panties in your in-tray or a telltale stain on your clothing that you attribute to spilt Tipp-Ex.

3. Don't use the company email
There are two concerns here. The first is forgetting to delete an incriminating email and someone viewing it on screen. The other is accidentally sending an email congratulating your lover on his/her sexual prowess to 'All Staff'.

4. Avoid coming to work in the exact same clothes two days running
This is a sure-fire sign that a) you're a slob, or more likely, b) you didn't make it home the night before. Rumours will fly before you can say, 'Reprehensible behaviour.'

5. Avoid relationships with junior staff
You have so much more to lose than the busty office intern or that hunky guy who works in the mailroom, both of whom could resort to blackmail if you try and end the affair – or just because they can. For this reason affairs should only be conducted with those colleagues on an equal or higher pay grade.

6. Be professional at all times

Maintain a work-like demeanor at all times. For example, avoid calling your co-worker 'Honeybuns' or 'Babe', blowing kisses across a crowded boardroom table or doodling both your initials in a love heart on a meeting agenda.

7. Flirt discreetly

Discretion is the key to a successful affair. Subtle flirting allows you to maintain your professionalism and secrecy over your relationship. Stealing a furtive glance over the photocopier or brushing past someone in a corridor is far more acceptable than doing it doggie-style on your desk.

8. Choose rendezvous points far from the prying eye

Arrange your rendezvous points with as much care as Jason Bourne, rehearsing cover stories and escape routes. An empty stairwell where you can easily hear people approaching is far better than the stationery cupboard, where an impromptu groping session is almost certainly going to be interrupted by someone on the hunt for staples.

9. Don't show public displays of affection

To guarantee discretion, kissing, hugging and touching below the waist should only take place if the following three criteria are met:

• You're both on your own.
• There's no danger of co-workers seeing, hearing or approaching.
• You're outside the range of security cameras.

10. Avoid romantic liaisons in the lift

The sudden movement, the confined space, the mirrors on the walls… a liaison in a lift can turn from intrigue to misery in the space of just two floors. While the uncertainty of the doors opening in the middle of a romantic clinch can add a certain frisson to a clandestine relationship, ask yourself the following question: Do you really want to risk the HR director walking in on the middle of 'that' act?

11. Use code

If it's difficult to get private time at work devise a code system that will enable you to converse freely while keeping your relationship a secret. For example, 'report' could mean 'quickie' while 'field visit' might be 'the Travelodge down the road'. Ensure you both understand the code otherwise being asked by your paramour if you want to stay behind to 'reconcile capital expenses and inventory valuations' could result in a very boring evening.

12. Don't flaunt it

It might be a real ego boost but resist the temptation of uploading your sex tape to the company intranet.

29

Forgetting someone's name at a social occasion

Most of us know what it's like meeting someone you know on a social or professional basis and having to greet them – or worse still, introducing them to someone else – and realising to your horror that you've completely forgotten their name.

You're certain it's John. Or Jim. Or it might be James. Or Ricky. Then again was it Kevin? Or Cindy? Fear not. There are a number of proven techniques that will enable you to come out of this situation with your credibility and dignity intact:

NAME AMNESIA: SEVEN WAYS TO OVERCOME THIS AFFLICTION

1. Admit it

It might seem like the obvious tactic but it's the coward's way out. Sure, it says, 'I'm honest', but it also says, 'I'm an idiot'. Use only as a last resort.

2. Keep it generic

Greet the mystery person by an affectionate name that you can pass off as a believable term of endearment. These greetings are best accompanied by a gentle punch to the shoulder.

For Men	For Women
Bud	Babe
Daddy-O	Doll/Doll Face
Dude	Honey Bunny
Man	Sweetie/Sweetie Pie/Sweetums
Old Chap	Sugar Lumps
Hombre	Sister
Romeo	Boo
Moose	Muffin pants
El Capitano	Angel/Angel Face
Bro	Cupcake
Big Guy	Princess
Studosaurus	Sex Kitten

3. The cool handshake

The familiarity with which you deliver this handshake is usually enough for the person with no name to believe without any doubt that you really remember them. Smile and put your hand out in greeting, but rather than execute a conventional handshake, perform a series of intricate hand manoeuvres using a combination of the following:

- High-fives
- Fist punches
- Palm slaps
- Back-of-hand slaps
- Grasping wrists
- Locking thumbs

- Bending elbows, cupping right hands and bumping chests together
- Making a gun with your fingers, firing it and blowing away the smoke

Note: End the routine by saying, 'Boo-ya!'

<u>Important</u>

Avoid the use of more than 3 body parts.

Keep the use of the lower body to a minimum.

Avoid a high-ten since this just looks like you're playing patty-cake.

Avoid Jazz Hands. You're greeting someone, not auditioning for *Chicago*.

---

4. The mock fighting diversion

An alternative to the above. As the person approaches duck your head, do some fancy footwork and throw a couple of mock punches. Immediately follow this by smiling, then give a bear hug like you're greeting a long-lost friend.

Note: This technique is best used on men.

5. Deduce it from their email address

Rather than greet the person by name, say something like: '*Hey! Good to see you again. You know what, I realised I lost your email address!*' After the person gives you their email address you can work out their name, thank them and then continue to use their name a few more times to reinforce the impression that you knew it all along.

Note: This will not work in all circumstances. For example, it is doubtful whether the person talking to you was actually christened 'Hotlips443' or 'bigfella26'.

6. Guess

Always worth a shot. It's a numbers game so go for one of the most common names like Mike, Richard, David, Robert, Andrew, Helen, Lisa, Emma, Michelle or Sarah. Unless you feel particularly lucky avoid Suri, Nebuchadnezzar, Titus, Latondra or Agnes.

7. Claim you have Alzheimer's

A straightforward excuse to explain your temporary memory loss. However, to make it convincing ensure you demonstrate other effects of the condition. For example, forgetting where you live, what you do for a living or that you have to remove your outer garments before going to the toilet.

30

Leaving a party early

Unless you've been invited to a formal social gathering that has a designated start and end time, usually expressed by something quaint like 'Carriages at 11pm', the important thing to remember about most parties is there are absolutely no rules. * That means you can arrive and leave any time you damn well want. It's only social convention and a fear of upsetting the host that makes us stay long after the fun/novelty has ended – but it doesn't have to be this way...

* Even 'Bring a bottle!' is a request, and despite what your host might say or think, it cannot be legally enforced.

Sometimes you just know when it's time to leave a party.

YOU KNOW IT'S REALLY TIME TO LEAVE A PARTY WHEN...

- The host says, 'OK, it's time to watch the wedding video!'
- The host says, 'OK, it's time for the *Annie* singalong!'
- The entertainment involves either board games or Class-A drugs.
- All the other guests are fat and naked and disappearing into bedrooms in pairs.
- All the alcohol has run out and all that's left to drink is milk, Ribena or vase water.
- The most attractive person there looks like Susan Boyle.
- Someone starts to draw a pentangle on the carpet.
- The guy/girl you had your eye on is currently swallowing the tongue of someone else.
- The music consists of Coldplay, Snow Patrol, Ed Sheeran and Little Mix on endless rotation.
- It's 11pm and everyone is stone cold sober.
- The main topics of conversation are the dearth of good au pairs and skiing in Chamonix.
- Your ex is walking towards you carrying both a grudge and a kitchen knife.
- You're being propositioned by the host's dad.

ESCAPE METHODS

The Semi-Terminator
Step 1: Tell your host you're just popping out but just like Arnie, you'll be back.
Step 2: Leave.

Step 3: Don't come back.

Ghosting (also known as the 'Parisian Goodbye')
Plain and simple – just walk out without saying goodbye. Difficult to do discretely if there are less than 10 people present, but in any larger gathering there's a good chance no one will notice you're missing. When ghosting, exit as quietly as possible, making sure you have your coat and/or bag. There's nothing more awkward than having to do the Walk of Shame as you re-enter the party to retrieve your possessions.

Babysitter Trouble
A great Get-Out-Of-Jail-Free card to play if you're the parent of young children. Ensure your fake conversation includes one or more of these phrases:
• 'What do you mean "abducted"?'
• 'Hold him upside down until it falls out!'
• 'Well, you'll just have to suck out the poison.'
• '*Paranormal Activity 2*! How much of it did she watch?'
• 'How the hell can you mistake the bleach for lemonade?'
• Anything that includes the words 'fire extinguisher'.

Emergency Situation
The great thing about emergencies is that they're unpredictable. They could occur anywhere: while you're at work, at home, shopping, in transit, at the zoo, in church – or at a party. Especially at a party. Like Babysitter Trouble above, all you need is a fake phone conversation and a shocked countenance, explaining the nature of the emergency to your host in as few words as possible.

Important
1. Don't make the story too elaborate. This will just leave you open to cross-examination by your hosts and guests.
2. Temper the level of danger so the emergency is believable.
3. Ensure your story is unable to be collaborated.

Ten phrases to avoid in order to ensure your emergency sounds credible
- Zombie invasion
- Sinkhole
- Fiery Comet
- Psycho killer
- Anthrax
- Explosion
- Big Foot
- African killer bees
- Hostage
- Squidzilla

Sudden Dental Crisis
Most parties involve food of some description, which means there's the opportunity to blame crudités, hors d'oeuvres, vol-au-vents or other fancy-sounding party snacks for chipping your tooth or losing a filling. As you say goodbye, hold your mouth and grimace but remember to also glare accusingly at your host.

'I've got to change my dressing'
Just say these six words to your host. The expression will conjure 100 thoughts in their heads, most of them unpleasant and some repugnant, involving pus, and they'll be only too pleased to see you go.

31

Getting rid of unwanted houseguests at Christmas

There's nothing intrinsically wrong with relatives and friends coming together on Christmas Day and playing out some sort of Dickensian fantasy. The problem arises when the coming together takes place at your house – and you find your guests still there two days after Boxing Day, or on Twelfth Night. Christmas may be a time for peace and goodwill, but it's also the time for mooching.

Many houseguests feel that honouring you with their presence is adequate compensation for eating and drinking you out of house and home, and assume that just because they have nothing better to do over the holiday period, neither do you. Benjamin Franklin said 'fish and visitors smell in three days'. He was dead right.

HOW TO GET CHRISTMAS HOUSEGUESTS TO LEAVE OF THEIR OWN VOLITION

Make them feel uncomfortable
The two most effective methods of making guests feel awkward are nudity and support of ultra-right wing causes. Combine the two by walking around the house stark naked while vehemently making the case for Aryan supremacy.

Instigate psychological torture
Just as US 'psy-ops' teams have broadcast heavy metal or the theme from *Barney & Friends* incessantly at high volume to weaken the spirit and resolve of terrorist groups, you too can use this technique to destroy the will of houseguests – the will to stay longer than you want. Loudly and incessantly play tracks by David Gray, the Bee Gees or Barbra Streisand – or anything involving bagpipes.

Lay siege
Technically, you can't really lay siege to your own house while you're still in it. However, you can impose siege conditions on your guests by turning off the water so they can't wash or use the toilet, and throwing away all food. The novelty of being hungry, dirt-encrusted and wallowing in their own filth soon wears off.

Make them pay
Present a bill at the end of each day to cover your guests' share of the utilities and food bills, plus the use of a bed or their contribution to the mortgage. Their initial reaction will be one of amusement; however calling the police for non-payment will soon wipe the smile from their faces.

113

Make them work

In exchange for your hospitality insist houseguests perform a number of demeaning or dangerous household chores. This could be anything from getting rid of the wasps' nest in the eaves, unclogging the drains by hand or removing the decomposing rat that's stinking out the attic.

Smoke 'em out

Imagine your houseguests are badgers or skunks but instead of using smoke to get them to leave the property, which may well invalidate your house insurance as well as making the curtains pong for days afterwards, use a combination of unpleasant festive smells including turkey curry, burnt pigs in blankets, rancid feta cheese and damp dog (and yes, feta cheese *is* a festive food – well, in Greece, that is).

Xmas quiz

Houseguests like nothing better than to play games, so tell them you've found this great Christmas quiz with a difference: wrong answers will result in a series of compulsory forfeits. They'll think this will be a bit of fun until they learn that a) the forfeits all involve leaving the house immediately and b) the questions have been prepared by Dr Stephen Hawking, Noam Chomsky and Malcolm Gladwell.

Freeze 'em out

Turn off all the heating and announce, 'Well, someone's got to take a stand against those faceless money-grabbing energy conglomerates.'

Go Amish

If freezing them out doesn't work, announce solidarity with

your Amish brethren and turn off the electricity, wear a black hat and speak with a German dialect. Refuse all contact with your houseguests, or as you now call them, 'the English'.

Noisy sex
Embarrass your guests into leaving by either engaging in, or faking, noisy sex. If the latter, leap up and down on your bed and rattle the headboard while yelling these phrases at random intervals:

'Now the other hole!'

'It's your turn to be (insert name of houseguest).'

'I love you, Mother.'

My House, My Rules
Tell your guests that as long as they're under your roof, they have to abide by your rules, even if these include the following:
• An 8pm curfew
• No trousers indoors
• Only watching programmes featuring Davina McCall

Hold a Jennifer Aniston DVD marathon
Lock the lounge door and ramp up the volume as you play a succession of her starring roles – for example, *Along Came Polly*, *Friends with Money*, *The Break-Up*, *Love Happens*, *The Bounty Hunter* and *The Switch*. If your guests aren't ready to pack up and leave after *He's Just Not That Into You*, they're already dead.

Pretend you're a werewolf
All you need to do:
a) Tell your guests in hallowed tones that it's a family curse.
b) Howl plaintively after everyone else has gone to bed.

32

Ordering off a foreign menu

There are few things than can make you feel as socially inadequate and inept as having to order from a foreign menu. It's worse still if you're with a date or someone else you're trying to impress and you're under pressure from a supercilious waiter who's taking immense pleasure in your ignorance and the fact that you'll probably order the curried goat ears.

So how do you appear urbane and worldly when you can't pronounce any of the dishes, let alone understand what culinary abominations hide behind their foreign names? Get it wrong and you're in big trouble. Order *nóżki* in a Polish restaurant and you'll be served a plate of jellied pig trotters, while ordering *stracotto d'asino* in an authentic Italian trattoria will get you a bowl of donkey stew. Many other foreign dishes (far too many to list here) combine offal with two other types of offal…

Depending on the language, some danger words are easy to recognise. See the words *intestin* or *testicules* on a French menu and you've got a pretty good idea what to expect… but what if you've been taken to a Vietnamese restaurant and the waiter is enthusing about *tủy sống*? No one wants to eat a dish containing spinal cord. Not even if it's one of the specials…

KNOW YOUR FOREIGN DISHES: A FOOLPROOF GUIDE TO AVOIDING EATING OFFAL, SEXUAL ORGANS OR PETS

Use the handy guide on the next page to determine if any curious-sounding dishes are likely to offend your morals or your taste buds.

TYPE OF CUISINE	Testicles	Intestines	Blood	Brain	Spleen	Spinal cord	Cat
French	testicules	intestin	sang	cerveau	rate	moelle épinière	chat
German	hoden	gedärme	blut	gehirn	milz	Rückenmark	katze
Italian	testicoli	intestino	sangue	cervello	milza	midollo spinale	gatto
Spanish	testículos	intestinos	sangre	cerebro	bazo	médula espinal	gato
Polish	jądra	jelita	krew	mózg	śledziona	rdzeń kręgowy	kot
Hungarian	herék	belek	vér	agy	lép	gerincvelő	macska
Mongolian	Төмсөг	гэдэс	цусны	тархи	дэлүү	нугасны	муур
Vietnamese	tinh hoàn	ruột	máu	não	lá lách	tủy sống	mèo
Turkish	hayalar	bağırsaklar	Kan	beyin	dalak	omurilik	kedi

33

Cannibalism: know your table manners

'Table manners' might be a misnomer; any scenario where you must resort to cannibalism in order to survive means you're unlikely to have a table – for example, if you've survived a plane crash in the Andes or a desert, and your 'five a day' consists of victims from the disaster. However, for the purpose of this section, we'll assume you do have a table (even if this is a piece of shattered cabin fuselage balanced on two boulders) and similarly, an improvised napkin and plate.

It really doesn't matter whether you're tucking into a tender piece of chicken breast, a leg of lamb or a human thigh, diners should always adhere to an established eating etiquette. Just because you're living like a savage doesn't mean you have to eat like one...

Unfamiliar food
Unless you've tried cannibalism before, most of the food you'll be eating will be unfamiliar and you might not be sure

*It's good
manners never
to chew small
intestines with
your mouth
open.*

of the correct way to eat it; for example, should eyeballs be chewed or swallowed? There are three ways to proceed: (a) Wait until someone else starts to eat and follow suit, (b) Ask someone how the food should be eaten, or (c) Avoid the food altogether.

Dealing with food you don't want

Although your very survival rests on eating other people, there might be some things you don't want to try. Not everyone is partial to tucking into a loved one's bottom or spleen. It's good manners to try all of the dishes served even if all you take is a single bite. In this case leave the remaining food at the side of your plate. Your fellow diners are bound to be ravenously hungry and the food is unlikely to be wasted.

Napkins

Good manners dictate that you should place your napkin in your lap and not tuck it into your shirt collar like a baby's bib. Although it can protect your clothes from spillages, the napkin's main purpose is to enable you to seamlessly remove offal and bloodstains from the sides of your mouth.

When to start eating

Hot body parts should be consumed while they're still hot. That means that if flesh or organs are cooked, it's acceptable to begin when two other diners have been served. If the flesh or organs are being consumed raw, then it's polite to wait until everyone is seated.

Elbows

The only elbows that can be rested on the table are those served as the entrée.

Passing food
Body parts should always be passed to the right.

Reaching
Reaching across the table or into another diner's personal space is frowned upon. If anything is beyond your normal reach ask the person closest to the item for assistance, saying for example, 'Do you mind passing me the fried pancreas?'

Seasoning food
Good table manners dictate that you taste your food before seasoning it. Hastily covering a piece of fricasséed oesophagus with black pepper or drowning it in ketchup implies you have automatically assumed that the cook's creation needs improving on.

Eating quietly
The essence of good table manners is unobtrusiveness since noise impedes conversation. Loudly gnawing on a pelvis or sucking the marrow out of a thighbone is both unpleasant to listen to and considered impolite.

The last portion
Do not take the last testicle (for example) without first offering it to all the other diners. Only when everyone declines should you then help yourself.

Excusing yourself
Eating human flesh or organs can be disagreeable on both moral and taste grounds. If you feel particularly nauseous excuse yourself from the table, placing your napkin loosely folded *on your chair* – or what passes for a chair (and which might in

fact just be the ground). This indicates you'll be returning after being violently sick.

Leaving your napkin loosely folded to the *left of your plate* indicates you have finished and are not returning. This might be because you're full up – or possibly because you're so disgusted with your barbaric behaviour that you're going outside the camp to cry inconsolably and then kill yourself.

Giving a toast
Given the fact that you're having to eat dead people, your future is probably quite bleak – and it's unlikely you'll have anything at all to toast or celebrate (the likelihood of being rescued is, of course, minimal). However, it's good manners and a sign of respect to toast the victim you're currently devouring.

Asking for seconds
Don't! The number of bodies should have been carefully rationed and taking second helpings of caramelised ears or ankle cutlets will upset the delicate balance between salvation and starvation.

Letting someone know they have food in their teeth or on their face
Be subtle and discrete; don't bring it to the attention of everyone at the table and don't embarrass the person. For example, point to your chin and whisper, 'Excuse me, you might need to use your napkin', rather than, 'There's a piece of brain matter stuck in your beard'.

Finding a hair in your food
This is the least of your worries.

ALSO REMEMBER...

- Never chew small intestines with your mouth open.
- It's considered bad manners to play a rib cage like a xylophone while others are still eating.
- Do take photos of your food. This will be invaluable for your book in the rare eventuality that you're actually rescued.

34

Breaking a curse

So you've done something wrong. In most cases this will result in you being reprimanded, shunned, dumped, sacked, sued, imprisoned or punched, or a combination. In some extreme cases, however, the person you wronged won't rely on social exclusion or the legal system for punishment: they'll just curse you.

We're not talking about them calling you a fuckwit or similar, we're talking about them invoking the black arts to inflict harm. Call it a curse, a hex, a jinx or even spiritual poisoning... it's not nice. And unlike a tickly cough, a curse is unlikely to respond to anything you can buy over the counter at Boots.

However, before you can take action you need to assess whether the bad things that have been happening to you are the result of black magic – or just because you're clumsy, unlucky or pissed. Falling down stairs, for example, could be the result of any of those states.

THESE PEOPLE CAN CURSE YOU	THESE PEOPLE PROBABLY CAN'T
• Voodoo priests • Romany gypsies • Witches/Wizards/ Sorcerers/Shamans • The descendant of an Ancient Egyptian priest • Satan	• Your boss • Your ex • Your mother-in-law • Under-tipped restaurant staff • Your grouchy neighbour

TELLTALE SIGNS YOU MAY HAVE BEEN CURSED

1. Inexplicable health problems
These could be anything from allergies, hair loss, bad breath, nagging headaches, unexplainable aches and pains or urine the colour of Pepsi Max.

2. Nightmares
Persistent or recurring bad dreams could be a sign that an enemy has gained access to your mind. Habitual visions of being poisoned by a snake or scorpion, or being sodomised by Lucifer, are common indications that you've been cursed. Either that or you're mentally ill.

3. Dark omens
Seeing 3 crows cawing in a graveyard or 3 jet-black dogs in the street staring ominously at you… these are never good signs.

If you have good reason to believe you've been a victim of the black arts, don't despair…

WAYS TO BREAK YOUR CURSE

Cast your own spell

There are far too many curse-breaking spells to cover within this book. Google 'Spells to break a curse' and you'll find over half a million entries; however, it's important to note that these are not all straightforward. Many of them involve the following:

- Obscure and hard-to-obtain herbs.
- Consecrated black candles.
- Graveyard dirt.
- Knowing the date of the waxing moon.
- Burying objects somewhere on the property of the person who has cursed you.
- Digging up the same said objects at a later date, then burning them.

Results: Two things could happen from casting one of these spells; either the curse will be lifted or you'll be arrested for trespassing.

Make an incantation

Like spells, there's an equally inexhaustible list of incantations you can make – many of which seem to involve a lighted candle, a rabbit's foot charm and being outdoors at midnight.

Effective incantations usually involve these phrases:
- 'If truly jinxed or cursed I am, set it free with quench of flame.'
- 'With rabbit's foot and magic verse I banish now this wicked curse.'

- 'By thrice repeating this enchanted spell, I return the hex to the gates of Hell.'

Ineffective incantations usually involve these phrases:
- 'Hey presto.'
- 'Do you like green eggs and ham? I do not like them, Sam-I-am.'
- 'Give me a sign... Hit me baby one more time.'

Praying

This is a straightforward technique... just ask your god to remove the curse. To improve the chances of this happening it helps to also beg forgiveness for any wrongdoing and promise to modify your future behaviour.
Note: The simplicity of this technique should be balanced with the fact that it is bound to fail.

Appeal to the curser's better nature

It's important to note the fact that someone has put a curse on you in the first place is an indication that they probably don't have a better nature. Still, worth a try if all else fails.

Casting your own curse

It's reassuring to know that there are more than fourteen times as many search-engine entries for casting a curse than spells to break them. Two wrongs don't make a right, but casting a hex on your enemy can make you feel better.

35

How to avoid alien abduction

Whether you believe in UFOs or are a true sceptic, you have to admit that being abducted by an extraterrestrial life form could be very unsettling. No one likes being woken from a deep, satisfying sleep to have a shiny metal probe inserted up their nose or into their anus – let alone being impregnated without any form of foreplay. And then there's the stigma that surrounds you afterwards and its effect on relationships with loved ones or co-workers. After all, sounding off in the office pub at lunchtime about being teleported to Zeta Reticuli is likely to severely limit your promotion prospects.

While not foolproof, the following methods will limit the chances of abduction and any subsequent social ostracisation.

SIX WAYS TO STAY SAFE

1. Avoid locations where you're likely to be abducted
Apart from your bedroom, most alien abductions take place

in the middle of nowhere. Aliens tend to avoid locations where there are many witnesses, so try and spend your leisure time in crowded places like busy bars, clubs or restaurants. Avoid locations where you'll be alone, such as walking across the local heath at night or at the cinema watching an Adam Sandler retrospective.

2. Set your alarm clock to sound at random intervals

Most alien abductions take place when the victim is in a deep sleep. To avoid this, take steps to wake yourself up in the middle of the night or early morning. The advantage is that being awake will make you less susceptible to abduction. But the disadvantage is that chronic lack of sleep makes you more susceptible to depression, heart disease, strokes and diabetes, as well as feeling very crotchety.

3. Control your thoughts

Aliens are able to read minds, so as far as it's possible, avoid any conscious or subconscious thoughts that might imply that you're ready and ripe for abduction. Thoughts to avoid include being teleported on board a flying saucer, having a shiny metal object inserted somewhere it shouldn't be, or being impregnated by a Star Child.

4. Make life difficult for them

Be obstructive in both senses of the word. Blocking your rectum will frustrate their attempts to insert an anal probe. It's been well documented that aliens are likely to move on to a new victim rather than risk getting their fingers grubby and wasting precious time trying to remove a cork or any foreign object.

ALIEN ABDUCTION FAQs

Are some types of people more likely to be abducted?
Abductions can happen to anyone irrespective of intelligence, ethnicity or class. However there is a higher likelihood among those living in the backwoods, in trailer parks and with a large collection of UFO books.

Why would an alien want to abduct me?
Analysis of reported abductions shows there are four main reasons: to warn the victim about nuclear proliferation, to implant some form of biotelemetry device, to use them as hosts for a human/alien hybrid or merely because they want to touch their bottom.

Is it possible to fight off aliens?
In some circumstances yes (see above); however, using violence on an alien should be a last resort. If extraterrestrials can travel millions of light years through space or master inter-dimensional teleportation then it's highly likely they will have weapons at their disposal that will really hurt.

Are homemade 'thought screen' helmets fashioned from tin foil effective?
Yes, but only in making you look like an unemployed nut-job conspiracy theorist.

I can't account for six hours missing from my life – does that indicate I was abducted?
Possibly. That or you were playing Neknominate.

If I'm taken aboard an alien spacecraft can I claim air miles?
Go away·

5. Sleep with a dog in your bedroom

Generally speaking, aliens tend not to abduct victims with dogs. Apart from your pet barking and raising the alarm, many extraterrestrials are actually allergic to fur. Strangely, for all their advanced technologies like anti-matter propulsion and plasma energy beams, aliens have not yet realised how simple it is to cause a diversion with a string of sausages.

6. Use physical force

If it's possible, strike out at the aliens in order to disorientate them and make your escape. Their large almond-shaped eyes are the best targets. Although your instinct might be a sharp kick to their groin in an attempt to bruise their testicles, our knowledge of alien biology is very limited and we cannot assume that aliens a) even have testicles or b) if they do, where they are located. For all we know the alien's scrotum could be behind its knee, hanging from an armpit or at the back of its throat. Don't take chances, go for their big bug eyes.

36

Breaking up with a werewolf

As the song goes, 'Breaking up is hard to do'. But breaking up with a werewolf is harder... and a lot more worrying.

An acrimonious split with an ordinary boyfriend could result in some snide comments on Facebook or a refusal to hand back your favourite CDs. Dumping a werewolf, however, could result in having your entrails clawed out, so it's important that you consider the split carefully before announcing your intentions.

ASK YOURSELF: DO I REALLY WANT TO SPLIT UP WITH MY WEREWOLF BOYFRIEND?

Reasons to split up

- You hate having to arrange date nights around the lunar calendar.
- It's such a bore having to vacuum your apartment every time he transforms.

Not sharing the same interests is one of the main reasons why relationships with werewolves can become strained

- Those scratches on your back really hurt.
- He always comes into the house with muddy feet...
- and poops in the garden.
- His idea of foreplay is humping your leg.
- He's always using your razor.
- There's only so many times you can snuggle up and watch
  The Howling.
- It's really embarrassing having to go to the doctor with
  worms.
- You want him sleeping in your bed, not at the foot of it.
- You get very anxious about love bites.
- All he wants to do is drink beer with his pack.
- He completely ignores you when you say, 'Get your paws
  off me!'
- He cheated on you with that golden retriever.

Reasons to stay together

- It's endearing having a boyfriend you can call 'fangy', 'furball'
  or 'killer'.
- You love his hairy chest.
- He's sooooo strong.
- Who'd want to split up with someone who looks like Taylor
  Lautner?
- You love it when he nuzzles your neck.
- Watching him scratch his ear with his big toe really makes
  you laugh.
- He has a five o-clock shadow at 7am... and it's *so* macho.
- You like doing it wolfie-style.

IF YOU REALLY FEEL YOU HAVE TO SPLIT UP...

1. Pick a good time
Timing is everything. The worst time you can announce your break-up is on the night of the full moon, when he's likely to be ravenously hungry. And the best time? Any other occasion.

2. Consider one of these break-up lines:
• 'Sorry, I've given you the bullet. Just be glad it's not a silver one (ha ha).'
• 'I'm sorry but howling isn't communicating.'
• 'I want a baby, not a puppy.'
• 'I gave you love, you gave me nits. This clearly isn't working.'
• 'I've got a fur allergy.'
• 'Watching you lick your own balls just doesn't do it for me.'
• 'We don't have anything common. I love running, cooking and rom-coms and you like ripping sheep apart with your bare hands.'
• 'I want to get married but all you want to do is mate.'
• 'I hate waking up next to you and finding half a dead squirrel in the bed.'
• 'I can't stand your mood swings.'

3. Be firm
Your werewolf boyfriend will probably say he can change.

Just remind him that this is the very reason you're breaking up in the first place.

37

Making a deal with Death

When your time's up, your time's up...
Well, not necessarily.

When the Grim Reaper appears in his black cowl, waiting for the last grain of sand to fall in his hourglass, it's often possible to negotiate with him for some extra time alive. Making a deal with Death is like entering any other form of negotiation – with one main exception. In most discussions you can enjoy a position of power by being able to walk away from the deal. This simply isn't the case with the Grim Reaper, who unfortunately enters any negotiations with the upper hand... and that hand is holding his scythe.

That said, there are still some crucial dos and don'ts that will help maximise your lifespan.

ADVICE FOR NEGOTIATING FOR LONGER LIFE

Check the Grim Reaper has the authority to sign off on a deal
Establish this at the beginning. You don't want to enter into protracted discussions only to find out that the final agreement needs to be validated by God, or even the Devil.

Make clear your objectives at the start of the negotiations
Be specific about what you want, i.e. when you are willing to die and by what means.

Never accept the Grim Reaper's first offer
His opening gambit will probably be, 'Right now. Heart attack.' Your response should be something along the lines of, 'In ten years' time. Being shot by a jealous husband.'

Know your bottom line
Start the negotiations with a clear understanding of the minimum deal you're prepared to make, i.e. you'll settle for 'Seven years' time. Lightning strike on the golf course'.

Be clear and concise in your objectives
Never use vague terms like 'approximately' or 'about' in your demands. Ask the Grim Reaper for 'between 5 and 10 years' extra life' and he'll always go for the minimum.

Stay calm
Appearing relaxed or even blasé about your demise will be very unnerving for the Grim Reaper and gives you an edge in negotiations.

Look for commonalities

When you share a common interest or find a common ground it's more difficult for someone to be in confrontation with you. In the course of your discussions try and find something you and the Grim Reaper have in common – for example, cancer, air crashes, the plague or heavy metal.

Look the Grim Reaper straight in the eye

OK, the Grim Reaper doesn't technically have eyes since he's a skeleton, but look deep into the sightless orbs of his skull when you negotiate so he knows you're deadly serious.

Retain your dignity

Although every instinct says cry, beg or whimper like a whipped dog, remain composed and professional at all times. Treat the conversation as if you are negotiating an extra discount on a sofa, not pleading for your life.

Say you understand the Grim Reaper's position

Show concern for his need to take your soul in order to meet his quota. That way he'll feel you have empathy for his task and likely to be more open to a deal.

Focus on the issues, not the personalities

Try and ignore the Grim Reaper's malevolent reputation, the feeling of abject fear and horror he provokes and the fact he has complete and utter power over every living thing. Dwelling on this will just weaken your position and make you soil your pants.

Observe his body language

Shuffling from foot to foot indicates the Grim Reaper is under time pressure to agree a deal and is likely to submit to your requests. A series of practise swings with the scythe indicates your time is limited.

Ask for the agreement in writing, there and then
A formal contract signed in blood is ideal. The minimum to settle for would be the terms handwritten on a piece of A4, signed by both parties in biro.

TRYING TO BEAT DEATH AT CHESS

If you've watched *The Seventh Seal* by Ingmar Bergman, you might have the idea you could play a game of chess with the Grim Reaper and that if you win, Death will leave you alone. Don't do it! Death has taken the souls of the best chess players throughout history, so he knows every winning technique and strategy from the queen's gambit to the Sicilian Defence. Not only that, but Death isn't above cheating ('accidentally' knocking over pieces with the folds of his cloak is a common ploy).

38

Retrieving your soul from the Devil

So you've sold your soul to the Devil.
Shit happens.

It probably seemed like a good idea at the time... a sure-fire way to become rich beyond your wildest dreams, get that assistant sales manager's job or get off with the girl who works in the Pound Shop. But now, as the pre-agreed time rapidly approaches when the Devil will appear in an evil-smelling, sulphurous cloud to claim your soul and damn you to an eternity in Hell, you're having second thoughts as to whether this was such a wise idea. The contract you signed in blood while standing at a crossroads under the full moon was pretty binding... but if you've changed your mind there are still a few things you can try to get out of it.

METHODS FOR EXTRACTING YOURSELF FROM THE DEAL

Hire a good lawyer

High street solicitors might be fine for dealing with matrimonial matters or executing wills but when it comes to taking on Beelzebub himself, it pays to deal with one of the larger law firms, who have partners experienced in soul retrieval and might be able to find a legal precedent. It could be, for example, that the soul wasn't yours to offer in the first place – it actually belongs to God. Or they might find a loophole that invalidates the contract – were you actually standing in the drawn pentagram or was one foot marginally outside of it?

Comments

This is a high-risk method as most lawyers are in league with the Devil and will probably throw the case on purpose.

Challenge Satan to a violin-playing contest

Take a leaf out of the book of country musician Charlie Daniels and challenge Lucifer himself to duelling violins... or any instrument in which you're proficient (except the recorder or castanets. Satan refuses to play these instruments since they undermine his position as Prince of Darkness). Traditionally, if the Devil loses the battle he is obliged to nullify your contract.

Comments

Before embarking on this sort of challenge remember that Satan has had thousands of years to perfect his musical skills and technique, and practice scales – whereas you might only be Grade 3 piano.

Challenge Satan to an arm-wrestling match

As above, but unless you're a proficient cage fighter or happen to be The World's Strongest Man (or Woman) you are likely to fail.

Comments

The Devil might be weaker than God but he's still pretty strong. Plus, he has a nasty temper.

Sell your soul to someone else

Do this in advance with a legally binding contract witnessed and countersigned by two independent witnesses. When the Devil turns up to ask for your soul just tell him that he needs to claim it from the new legal owner. This might be anyone from someone on whom you seek revenge to your budgie.

Comments

Many contracts specifically forbid soul re-selling. Check yours carefully to make sure it's possible.

Repent in advance

Go to church and tell a priest what you've done, then tell them you want to recite the Sinner's Prayer and accept Jesus Christ into your life as your Lord and Saviour.

Comments

This needs to be followed up by having your head anointed with oil, which can subsequently take at least two weeks' treatment with medicated shampoo to rinse it all out.

Pray

You can always pray to your god for forgiveness and salvation then ask him to save your soul in the final moments before the Devil harvests it.

Comments

Unlikely to work; use only as a last resort.

Shredding the actual contract

As straightforward as it sounds.

Comments

Rarely works... to release yourself from an unholy pact with the Devil the contract needs to be completely destroyed (see below).

Burning the actual contract

Just as straightforward as shredding.

Comments

Be warned. As the agreement is consumed by fire you'll be wracked by so much physical pain you'll wish you were dead anyway.

Deny all knowledge that you made the agreement in the first place

When the Devil appears and demands your mortal soul, act shocked and inform him that you think this is an oversight and probably some sort of administrative error.

Comments

Really? REALLY?

39

Exorcism etiquette

Baby showers, engagement parties, silver-wedding anniversaries... all these events pale into insignificance when compared to exorcisms. Sure, at the other events there might be the odd bit of projectile vomiting but it's highly unlikely you'll see any form of levitation, let alone someone masturbating with a crucifix.

Apart from being rare, exorcisms are very private and personal events, so receiving an invitation to one should be coveted. You may feel nervous, apprehensive even, about going along – after all, witnessing demonic possession can be quite unsettling. However, provided you know the right way to behave, you'll have an enjoyable time.

THE DO AND DON'TS OF EXORCISMS

Don't drink the Holy Water

This is an intrinsic and vital part of the ceremony, not a

If you are asked to assist in an exorcism it's vital you stay focused on the holy ritual.

refreshment. Drinks will traditionally be served immediately after the exorcism.

Do dress accordingly
A hat and waterproof clothing will protect you to some degree if the possessed victim spews vomit, blood or faeces in your general direction. In addition, wearing layers will help keep you warm when the room temperature inevitably plunges several degrees.

Don't take photographs
While the sight of someone levitating off their bed or walking up the walls and across the ceiling is bound to be a YouTube sensation, it's important to stay focused on the holy ritual. The same applies to taking selfies next to the demon Pazuzu.

Don't touch the walls
During some exorcisms they may start to bleed and you'll get your hands sticky.

Don't pay attention to what the demon says
It will speak through the victim and scream some very unpleasant things about you and your family, particularly your mother and her penchant for sucking cocks in Hell.

Do be prepared to assist
You may be called upon to lend a hand in the proceedings with things like re-tying the victim to the bed or knocking him/her down from the ceiling with a broom.

Do stay calm
Seeing the victim rotating their head 360 degrees or talking in

a guttural growl can be alarming and upsetting. Stay composed; panic helps no one.

Don't chant inappropriately
Not only should you understand when to chant and when to stay silent, ensure the chants are appropriate, i.e. they should be extracts from the 'Rite of Exorcism'. Chanting frivolously, for example, in support of your football team, will lead the demon to believe you are an ally.

An example of a good chant:
'The power of Christ compels you!'

An example of a bad chant:
'There's only one Luis Suárez, one Luis Suárez…'

Don't yell, 'Take me!' near the end of the ritual. Not even for a laugh.
Demons are not known for their sense of humour or their appreciation of sarcasm and as soon as they hear this, will possess you in a heartbeat. If they had hearts…

40

Post-apocalypse dress code

A thermo-nuclear holocaust, a direct hit by a stray asteroid or a virulent global pandemic... the way the world ends isn't important. What is, however, is how survivors will cope in this post-apocalyptic landscape – one where hardship, violence, pain and chaos will reign – a future where gangs and individuals will savagely hunt and kill each other for the world's ever dwindling resources and where one group in particular will feel the impact most: the post-apocalyptic fashionistas.

Frighteningly, they'll have to adapt to a society where not only has social order ceased to exist, but so too have *Vogue* and *GQ*. They'll need to survive in a world where the 'Mad Max' look will be every year's 'must have' and a shopping trolley will be the fiercest new accessory; a world where carrying last season's automatic pistol is an inexcusable fashion faux pas.

If you do survive, then no matter how starving you are, or how gangrenous your wound, it's more important than ever to remember the old adage, 'If you look good, you'll feel better'.

POST-APOCALYPSE FASHION TIPS

Match your leathers
Patent, grained, suede, nappa, distressed... leather comes in many finishes but if you want to be the most stylish survivor on the block ensure your jacket, coat, footwear and belt complement each other. Want to really impress? Also match your wallet and tactical backpack.

Button etiquette
Regardless of the ambient temperature, the bottom button of a coat or jacket is NEVER done up. Ever. Not even if you're trying to survive a nuclear winter or a new ice age.

Hats
Since you'll be spending most of your time outdoors battling the elements trying to find supplies or other groups of survivors, a post-apocalyptic world is likely to see a resurgence in hat wearing among men, but remember the hat needs to balance out your whole look. It's all about getting the proportion right, so the hat doesn't overpower you. Berets, baseball caps and beanie hats combine practicality with style – but avoid a flat cap. This will make you look less like a badass survivor and more like a Mumford & Sons tribute act.

Camouflage
No longer the de rigueur uniform of the homeless or Care in the Community patients, 'camo-wear' is an acceptable alternative to the leather look. However, like the latter, ensure consistency in your style – for example, don't mix and match Afghanistan camouflage with the Desert Storm look.
Note: Avoid the heavy foliage ghillie suit at all costs! Few people

can carry it off and you'll just resemble some sort of weird atomic-mutated swamp creature.

Double denim
Despite the durability and versatility of this material, wearing jeans with a denim jacket is still a definite fashion no-no, even if you're the last person on Earth (which, in fact, you might be).

Colours
If camouflage doesn't suit your skin tone, stick to neutral colours such as grey, taupe, olive green, cappuccino or tundra in order to blend in with your surroundings. Black has the advantage of complementing most colours as well as flattering your figure, and enables you to look chic and classic in even the most bleak or inhospitable conditions.

Ties
Don't think of your tie as a noose, think of it as an expression of individuality. Your choice of tie should say, 'I survived the meteor', 'Me 1, Bird Flu 0' or 'I looted Armani'. A wide tie looks traditional, so go for the slim look to represent the new world order.

Shoes
In a post-apocalypse world it's acceptable for footwear to combine protection with style; for this reason, combat, hiking or safety boots are an acceptable alternative to shoes for men as well as women as long as they are a darker shade than your trousers. *Note*: This will be the *only* time where 'sturdy' is an acceptable part of the fashion lexicon.

Accessories
These can add a glam note to the outfit and complete your

look. As with leather, match your metals: never wear a rose gold watchstrap if you're carrying a stainless steel hunting knife.

Guns

Despite the catwalks of New York, London, Paris and Milan probably being destroyed in a fireball there's still room in the post-apocalyptic world for fashionistas to seek status – however this won't be through clothes but firearms. In this new world your gun will say more about you than any designer logo. A Heckler & Koch MP5 says you're lively and high-spirited while a retro Uzi SMG says you're comfortable and confident in your own skin. *Note*: No wardrobe is complete without an LBS (Little Black Semi-automatic).

Socks

These should be made from natural fibres (wool, cashmere or silk) and must be darker than your shoes. Novelty socks are only acceptable in private. Sporting these in other situations, such as scavenging for food or setting a snare trap, will result in people thinking you're not really taking the whole 'survivalist' thing seriously.

HOW TO RECOGNISE IF YOU'RE IN A POST-APOCALYPTIC SITUATION

Type of Apocalypse	Visual clues
Plague/global pandemic	A 10 month wait just to see your GP. EBay crashes due to the demand for gas masks.
Collision with a meteor	Depending where it hits, either tidal waves or a massive dust cloud that obliterates the sun. A run on swimwear or sweaters.
Nuclear holocaust	Melting flesh. The term 'Smart casual' now means a radiation suit.
Alien invasion	The White House gets blown up. Ugly-looking slimy alien overlords with tentacles. Lots of laser beams.
Catastrophic climate change	You can see the sea... and you live in the Sudan. Anxious-looking penguins. Travel agents rushed off their feet. Your next-door neighbour is building an ark.
Machines take over the world	Armies of red-eyed, shiny mechanised killing machines stalking the land. Demoralised rag-tag humans living under-ground. A heroic resistance fighter who travels back to the past.
The Earth's core overheats	Even more small talk about the weather. Cornetto sales go through the roof. Boots sells factor-3000 sun tan lotion.
Divine Rapture	The world almost destroyed by an immense earthquake. The faithful rise up in the sky to met Jesus. Lots of people hurriedly change their religion.

41

Discovering a grizzly bear in the confessional box

Going to confession and admitting you've committed a mortal sin takes a certain degree of courage. Going there and discovering that a grizzly bear has somehow found its way into the other side of the confessional box requires even greater bravery – especially when you realise that the only thing that separates you from 363kg (800lb) of angry killing machine is a flimsy plywood partition.

Grizzly bears have very little interest in hearing about your transgressions, even those involving juicy sins like coveting your neighbour's wife. They are far more concerned with finding food or defending their cubs – and they rarely let anything hinder their progress. If you do find yourself in this situation stay calm and avoid sudden movements that the bear might mistake for aggression. Ignore this advice and you risk ending up closer to God (but not in a good way).

*Be warned. Grizzly
bears are more likely to
rip your face off than
listen sympathetically
to your transgressions.*

FIVE SIGNS THAT YOU MIGHT BE CONFESSING TO A GRIZZLY BEAR, NOT A PRIEST

1. As you approach the confessional box you notice a huge pile of steaming animal droppings on the altar and claw marks on the crucifix.
2. You say 'Forgive me, Father, for I have sinned', and the response is a bellowing roar.
3. Very few priests can run at up to 35mph (even when in pursuit of a choir boy).
4. Grizzly bears are more likely to eat you than ask you to recite three Hail Marys.
5. Instead of receiving the Sacrament of Reconciliation you get your face torn off.

WHAT TO DO TO SAVE YOUR LIFE

- Despite what you might have seen on the Discovery Channel, realise that meeting a real-life grizzly bear face to face is going to be far more terrifying than awe-inspiring.
- Grizzly bears have an incredibly acute sense of smell, so if you have any inkling that your priest might have been replaced by one do not under any circumstances take food into the confessional box with you. If bears can detect other animals upwind from 32 kilometres (20 miles) away they're sure to be able to detect an opened roll of wine gums in your jacket pocket from a distance of 0.6m (2ft).
- Unless you're an Olympic sprinter do not attempt to flee – just remain still and quiet and hope the bear

doesn't recognise you as a threat. In fact, don't just hope, pray.
- Don't play dead. The bear will take advantage of your apparent vulnerability and is more likely to rip your throat out than leave you alone.
- Resist the temptation to suddenly pull back the sliding screen between you to get a better look. It never pays to surprise a bear.

42

Waking up next to a complete stranger

You wake up much earlier than normal; it's still dark out. You yawn and stretch – then turn over so you can look at your alarm clock – but you can't see it. That's odd. For a few moments you lie there in a state of puzzled drowsiness and then the penny drops: you're not at home. But more worrying than not knowing your whereabouts is the fact that there's someone else in the bed. You suddenly remember having passionate sex with them but you have absolutely no idea who they are. To avoid acute embarrassment you must act fast.

Clues to the name of the bed's mysterious occupant will be in the house or apartment; it's just a case of looking for the evidence. And if that fails, there are some ingenious methods you can use to get this complete stranger to reveal his/her name...

FINDING OUT THEIR NAME WHEN THEY'RE STILL ASLEEP

The medicine cabinet

Find the bathroom and look in the medicine cabinet. There's bound to be an assortment of prescription medicines with your new lover's name on the label. If you're lucky it will have their full name, but even if it's just an initial and a surname, it's a start... although it might sound overly formal when she wakes up and you greet her with a cheery, 'Well, good morning, Miss S. Clarke'.

Note: If you see 'Azithromycin' on a medicine label it's not someone's exotic foreign-sounding name, it's an antibiotic for chlamydia.

The hall table

If you can make it further than the bathroom without waking your bedmate, look on the hall table for any discarded junk mail that would give you a clue to their name.

Note: Be sure the name on the envelope is accurate. No one likes being greeted as 'The Occupier'.

The toilet

Look through the reading matter kept in the toilet. If the stranger subscribes to magazines there's sometimes a name and address label stuck on the back cover. Not only will this give his/her full name but it will offer an insight into the sort of person you've just slept with.

Note: Make a speedy exit if you see any magazines about home surgery, coprophilia (obsessive interest in faeces) or bondage, or any with these words in the title: serial killer, Goebbels, gimp.

FINDING OUT THEIR NAME WHEN THEY'RE AWAKE

Ask how they spell their name
This is usually a win-win situation:
Outcome 1: If the name is unusual then you'll be rewarded with the answer – for example, 'Guinevere'.
Outcome 2: If the name is commonplace then you'll still be rewarded with the answer – for example, 'Don't you even know how to spell Susan?'

The magic trick
Step 1: Ask the stranger to write his/her name on a scrap piece of paper before handing it to you.
Step 2: Steal a glance at the name before crumpling the paper up into a tiny ball.
Step 3: Stare at the ball and say, 'Paperamus Teleportus'.
Step 4: Swallow it with a theatrical gulp and say, 'Well, Beatrice, I think you'll find a surprise if you look in your purse.'
Step 5: When they check their purse and the expected piece of paper isn't there, just shrug and say, 'Meh, what can you do?'

Ask them to text you their number
If you've only just met, chances are you won't have their number. If they're willing to give it to you, not only will you now have their number… you'll have their name too.
Note: Seeing that the sender of the text is 'Gill's Phone' means her name is Gill. It is highly unlikely that her surname is Phone.

Impersonate a police officer
Suddenly announce you're an undercover cop and whip out a fake police ID. Say you have to see their driving licence. Now.

After the stranger shows you, laugh and tell them you were just kidding! It's 50/50 that they'll think you're a joker or a weirdo.

Ask how their parents settled on such a great name

If the response is something like, 'Well, they were huge fans of Kylie Minogue', you've got the answer you want. On the other hand, 'I was named after my dad's mother' is not so helpful.

Scare them into revealing their name

While you're having coffee, scream and say you just saw a creepy masked figure at the window brandishing a bloody machete. They'll be so freaked out they'll call the police and say something like, 'Hello officer, it's Oceana Tuttle and I think my life might be in danger!' Or similar.

Note: It doesn't matter if you're in a twelfth-floor apartment. Masked figures are even creepier if they get around using suckers on the outside of a building.

Bring up childhood bullying

Go for the sympathy vote with this one. Just say, 'When I was growing up the kids at school used to really make fun of my name. Did they do the same with you?'

If you're lucky you'll get something like, 'No, even though I'm called Zaltana they left me alone'. If you're unlucky – and the stranger knows your name – you'll get something like, 'Why on earth would kids make fun of anyone called Jim?'

43

How to tell if your date is a man in drag

When you announce you're going out with Stephanie your mates snigger uncontrollably, but you dismiss it as petty jealousy. After all, she's a pretty girl, tall and toned, so it's natural they'll be jealous. There's something different about her – but you can't quite put your finger on it. Sure, you know she's a bit of a tomboy who likes a pint and a game of darts now and then, but there's something else. It's something imperceptible, something at the back of your mind that doesn't quite ring true, but you dismiss it. Maybe that little bit of mystery is behind the attraction.

The first date goes really well. She's entertaining, witty and smart – and you've got so much in common... Champions League football, car-tuning and Metallica. At the end of the evening you take her hands in yours to thank her for a lovely night. It's only then that you realise her hands are bigger than yours; then there's the hair on the back of her knuckles...

If this sounds like your experience the chances are that you've been dating a cross-dresser. There's absolutely nothing wrong with this; however, it's understandable that you may want a degree of clarity as to whether you're dating a woman, or a man dressed as one...

Don't jump to conclusions. Some women are very interested in Champions League football, car-tuning and Metallica.

HOW TO TELL A STEVE FROM A STEPHANIE

1. Does your date turn up wearing sweat pants?
☐ Yes ☐ No
'She' might be trying to conceal a telltale bulge. Or she might just be a slob. Either way, it doesn't bode well for a relationship.

2. Is your date reluctant to remove her scarf?
☐ Yes ☐ No
She could have something to hide. A love bite isn't really an issue; an Adam's apple is.

3. Are her shoulders wider than her hips?
☐ Yes ☐ No
Men's shoulders tend to be wider than their hips. Don't be taken in by any excuse involving retro eighties chic and shoulder pads.

4. Does she sound like Barry White?
☐ Yes ☐ No
It's important to recognise that Barry White's voice is only sexy when it comes from Barry White.

5. If you run your fingers through her long blonde hair does it come off in your hands?
☐ Yes ☐ No
A wig to disguise the effects of chemotherapy is OK. A wig to disguise the effects of male pattern baldness is not.

6. Was her choice of date movie *The Expendables 3* or *Fast & Furious 6*?
☐ Yes ☐ No
This might not necessarily be a sign that you're dating a man. It could mean you're dating an idiot.

7. Does your date wear excessive make-up?
☐ Yes ☐ No
This could disguise a multitude of sins such as spots, facial disfigurement or a five o'clock shadow.

8. Does her job involve welding, heavy lifting, cage fighting or donating sperm?
☐ Yes ☐ No
While there's much more gender equality in the workplace and it's bad practice to generalise, it is true to say that jobs involving manual labour, fighting or donating sperm do tend to be male-dominated roles.

9. Does she smell of creosote, Ronseal or 10/40 oil rather than Calvin Klein Obsession?
☐ Yes ☐ No
Despite what your date might say, female pheromones do not generally smell of things you'd find in a shed or garage.

10. Does she scratch her balls?
☐ Yes ☐ No

For your results, see overleaf.

Score

Count the numbers of times you ticked 'Yes'.

4 or less:

You're dating a woman. Probably.

5–7:

It's quite likely you're dating a member of the Russian shot-put team

8–10:

Sorry, but there's no doubt that you're dating a Mrs Doubtfire.

44

How to behave appropriately after a zombie outbreak

It's ironic that those who avoid being bitten in a zombie outbreak will have to survive in a dog-eat-dog world. Apart from having to push yourself physically in order to outrun and outfight hordes of the living dead, you'll also need to quickly re-assess your ethics and reset your moral compass. The world has changed and so must you.

That means it's now OK to shoot your best friend if you catch him awkwardly laughing off a bite-mark, saying, 'It's nothing', or battering a complete stranger to death over a tin of peaches. Polite society may have completely broken down but there will still be a need to know the correct way to interact with others.

This isn't just a question of manners, it's matter of survival.

THE NEW RULES FOR SOCIAL INTERACTION

Meeting other survivors

While it might be fun to join up with someone who loves the Kardashians as much as you, don't. You're not looking for friends, you're looking for a bunch of kick-ass people who can help you survive among the living dead. That means people who are handy with a bow and arrow, who drive a 4x4 or who have a tin opener. However, see 'Being trustworthy'...

Being trustworthy

Although trust is a priceless commodity in this uncertain future, be wary when meeting other survivors of the outbreak. Desperate times lead to desperate people; proceed with caution on the basis that any strangers you meet could very well mug or kill you just for a jar of pickled onions.

Positive discrimination

Actively seek out fat or asthmatic people. When being chased by a rampaging zombie horde it's important to remember that you don't need to outrun the zombies, you only need to outrun the slowest person in your group.

Being selfish

Sometimes your life can depend on what might otherwise be considered selfish or inconsiderate behaviour. 'Only the strong survive' is not true when you're being pursued. In these situations the only adage that counts is, 'Only those remaining upright survive'.

Remember, when push comes to shove, push.

Respecting the elderly
Don't think of the elderly as respected members of the community who should be valued for their wisdom, grace and fortitude. Think of them as zombie bait.

Staying loyal
In times like these it doesn't pay to get too attached to people. You might think that your partner is for life, but if he/she gets bitten or scratched, it's probably best to move on.

Let bygones be bygones
You haven't spoken to your neighbour for two years after he borrowed your lawnmower and broke it but when a zombie horde is ambling down your street it's time to put your differences behind you in the name of survival. Pool your resources to find either a means of escape or a safe refuge.

Be magnanimous
If someone wants to be a hero or make a name for themselves be the bigger man and let them have the glory. If you're among a gang of survivors stay at the back and don't volunteer for anything. Especially exploring an abandoned convenience store.

Keep morale high
Whether you're holed up in a cabin, a farmhouse or a basement, try and raise the spirits of any fellow zombie outbreak survivors by playing simple games, but do ensure any activities are uplifting and positive – pronouncing, 'I spy with my little eye something beginning with "Z"' is not such a good idea.

Stop caring what people think of you
Don't worry about garnering the respect of others. After a zombie outbreak you do what you have to do to survive, even if that means drinking from a toilet or ensuring the future of the human race by sleeping with your sister.

45

Blocking the toilet at someone's house

Until we evolve past the need to eat and defecate, or plumbing technology advances beyond the Victorian era, there will always be toilet blockages and these will always take place while you're at the home of your boyfriend/girlfriend, their parents, your boss or someone else you really need to impress.

The potential for embarrassment and complete social ostracisation is further exacerbated by the fact that most bathrooms nowadays are far more likely to feature an iPod dock than a plunger — a consequence of society putting more emphasis on entertainment than faecal removal.

This means if you *do* manage to block the toilet at someone's house you'll need to have the ingenuity and improvisational skills of Ray Mears and Bear Grylls in order to work out a method of disposing of the turd while retaining your dignity.

As they say, shit happens.

IS THERE A HIGH LIKELIHOOD THAT YOU'LL BLOCK THE TOILET?

- Is your nickname 'The Turdinator'?
- Does your portrait hang in the European Faecal Standards and Measurements Institute Hall of Fame?
- Have you just written: 'Dear Diary. It's now fifteen days since my constipation began…'
- Have you just taken part in a charity curry-thon?
- Are you carrying the norovirus?
- Did you recently eat two bars of Ex-Lax for a dare?
- Have you just returned from a holiday in Egypt?
- Do you have the *Guinness World Records* on speed dial?

If you've answered 'Yes' to any of these then it pays to take steps to minimise a potential toilet blockage…

Try a test flush
If it gurgles, you're probably going to have problems. But if it sounds like the Niagara Falls, you're good to go.

If you think a blockage is imminent
Flush halfway through your crap – or at least flush before you start wiping – then flush at the end. It's the combination of the turd AND the toilet paper that causes the blockage.
Note: Anyone within earshot will usually be too polite to ask why you've flushed twice. If they do, deny it and say it was an echo.

IF IT STILL WON'T FLUSH...

What you'll need
An implement to break up the turd and a restrictive sense of smell.

What to do
If cavemen could fashion knives out of an ox's jawbone then it should be within your ability to improvise a tool to cut the turd into small, flushable pieces. Look around the bathroom and see what you can use. A tub of hair sculpting wax? A liquid-soap dispenser? Cotton buds? Don't be stupid! None of these will be any help whatsoever. Look at the back of the door and see if there's a wire coat hanger – the poor man's Swiss Army Knife. If so, you're nearly home and dry. Squeeze the hanger so the two sides are parallel, about 20mm (1in) apart, and use a cutting motion to break up the turd before flushing again. After use, unbend it so it resembles, more or less, the original shape. Oh yes, rinse it under the tap before putting it back.
> *Did this work? If answer is 'no', continue.*

THE EMERGENCY PLUNGER

What you'll need
Guest towel, plastic bin liner from the waste bin; a sense of rhythm.

What to do
Wrap the towel around your fist and put your arm in the plastic bin liner. Insert your fist as far as it can go into the toilet bowl to create a tight seal – then start plunging with a regular in-out motion. In most cases the vacuum created will clear the blockage. Afterwards, carefully remove the bin liner, rinse and then replace it in the bin.

Note: Try not to rupture the bin liner. Explaining why the guest towel is covered in poo can be more awkward than the actual blockage itself.

> *Did this work? If answer is 'no', continue.*

MANUAL REMOVAL
What you'll need
Plastic bin liner from the waste bin or toilet paper; a good aim.

What to do
Using the bin liner or toilet paper, carefully remove the offending turd from the toilet bowl and throw it as far as you can out of the bathroom window. By the time it's found no one will associate the discovery with your visit and if the turd becomes separated from its wrapper it will probably be blamed on a neighbour's dog.

Note: Do not accidentally drop the turd as you prepare to throw it. Everyone knows the urban myth about one landing on the conservatory roof. Except it's not a myth.

> *If there's no window, continue.*

174

JUST LEAVE IT
No one wants to admit defeat but sometimes you can't fight nature; in this case all you can do is walk away from the disaster. As you exit the bathroom just say, 'Where I come from this is meant as a compliment to the host.'

Afterwards
Close your Facebook account immediately to prevent you seeing that your actions have gone from awkward social situation to viral public humiliation.

WARNING
If you're unable to locate a chain or a push-button flush it means you're probably about to defecate in the washbasin or the bidet.
Don't.

46

Going on a blind date with a vampire

You've finally completed your online dating profile as accurately and as honestly as you could: What's your favourite type of music? Are you a romantic at heart? Are you a spiritual person? Do you like change? Do you find it easy to express your feelings? Blah blah blah blah…

What you don't recall answering, however, is, 'Do you want to date the undead?' or ticking the box that indicated your ideal man would be 'between 800 and 1,200 years old'. Anyway, it's academic now as you find yourself on a blind date with a vampire.

Follow these guidelines and you'll have an enjoyable, relaxed time (or as relaxed as you can, going out with someone who has an unholy need to drink blood).

DOS AND DON'TS FOR YOUR VAMPIRE BLIND DATE

Don't pay too much attention to his/her profile photograph
The quickest way to ruin a blind date with a vampire is to walk in expecting Robert Pattinson and then feel disappointed when it's anyone *but* Robert Pattinson. There's no guarantee that your prospective partner's online photo is recent (or indeed, accurate), but there must be something about their personality and profile that took you this far, so go ahead with an open mind and you'll enjoy the occasion*.

* As long as he doesn't resemble Grandpa from *The Munsters*.

Don't set your expectations too high
This is your first meeting and it's just a chance to have fun and get to know each other. You'll be much more relaxed approaching it on this basis rather than telling yourself this is the night when you'll meet your soulmate and become an immortal vampire bride or bridegroom.

Do dress modestly
A date after work is best since you'll feel comfortable in your work clothes and won't be worrying whether you're wearing the wrong thing. However, if your date takes place at the weekend, go for smart casual. Avoid displaying too much leg, cleavage or, especially, neck.

Do focus on your date
Don't spend the whole evening talking about your job, your friends, your cat, etc., etc. Show interest in HIM or HER. It's not as though you're on a blind date with someone who works in data processing; a vampire will have plenty of interesting

things to talk about. Here are a few topics you may want to bring up: blood sucking, sunlight, fangs, coffins, wooden stakes, immortality and bats. That should keep you going.

Do be inquisitive

If you want this first date to be successful it's essential to keep the conversation going. Avoid closed-ended questions that only require 'yes', 'no' or 'I don't know' responses. Asking open-ended questions will stimulate a discussion and let them know you're interested ('So, what's the best thing about eternal life?').

Don't show off

You might be successful with a great job but drawing attention to it can be off-putting. If you're wearing expensive clothes and accessories, your date will notice; there's no need to flash your cash. Remember, it's actually quite difficult to impress someone who's immortal and who can fly.

Do offer compliments freely

It doesn't matter that your date might be centuries old and has probably seen and heard it all; any compliments offered must sound sincere and natural ('I just love what you've done with that cloak').

Do be open-minded

So you weren't expecting to date a vampire, but don't be too quick to judge. Acknowledge that we all have our funny little habits and idiosyncrasies and that chemistry can grow. Put your prejudices to one side when he tells you his hobby is bloodlust or you discover that she sleeps in a coffin full of the soil of her homeland.

Don't ask about previous relationships
There's a chance you might feel inadequate when your date
tells you about their affair with a member of the Russian royal
family in 1765 or how they dated Countess Elizabeth Báthory
in 1590.

Don't be afraid to laugh
Laughter will lighten the mood, especially if you're both feeling
a bit uncomfortable or tense, but humour should be natural.
Don't force it by asking your date if he's a bat-chelor, whether
she likes fang-furters, or if he's been to the Vampire State
Building.

Do show that you're considerate
Refrain from ordering anything with garlic. And irrespective of
your religious beliefs, don't wear a crucifix.

Do end the date on a good note
If you feel some sort of chemistry and attraction, that's great!
You can swap details and make arrangements to meet again. If
there's no magic there, or you really don't fancy going out with
the undead, then still make sure that you end the night positively
with a hug or maybe a peck on the cheek. They might not be
'the one', but that doesn't mean you have to be horrible to the
person in question at the end of the date.

Besides, it never pays to upset the Living Dead.

47

Being abducted by Somali pirates

One minute you're enjoying a well-deserved break on a chartered yacht in the Seychelles, relaxing after a delicious seafood lunch, gazing at the sailfish and marlin darting about in the crystal-blue waters. The next thing your boat has been boarded by Somali pirates, who overcome the crew and take over the bridge.

What was to become an afternoon's sunbathing or watching sea turtles now involves you being screamed at and manhandled by vicious-looking ex-militiamen brandishing AK-47s and machetes.

Being abducted and held hostage by Somali pirates can be a terrifying experience, so it's important to behave in the appropriate manner.

PIRATE KIDNAPPING: GUIDELINES

Don't try and escape
The Somali pirates who've taken control of your boat have

*Be careful. The Somali
pirates who take you
hostage may not share
your sense of humour.*

probably planned this operation over a long period and invested not only thousands of man-hours but also a considerable sum of money to make sure it's a success. Any escape attempt shows a complete lack of respect for their hard work and determination to succeed.

Don't whine
Be thankful you've been kidnapped by pirates and not a psychopath who wants to wear your skin as a cape, so stop whinging or complaining about your predicament. Concentrate on the positives: you're on a luxury yacht in the middle of the Indian Ocean, not tied and gagged in the back of a van or a basement-cum-torture chamber.

Respect their ambitions
Many of the pirates will be simple fishermen and ex-clan warlords who are just looking for a better way of life in their war-torn, poverty-stricken country. To thwart their plans is selfish, it's your continued status as a hostage that keeps their hopes and dreams alive.

Establish a rapport with your captors
If you can build some sort of bond with your captor, he'll generally be more hesitant to make you the first victim to be shot and thrown overboard if their demands aren't meant. Try and engage him in conversation. Useful topics include famines, civil war, former hostage Captain Phillips or the use of their country as a dumping ground for Russian weapons.

Don't insult your abductors
You may think the pirates are callous, repulsive, cold-blooded cowards for attacking civilians, but you should keep these

thoughts to yourself. Your abductors see themselves less as pirates and more as modern sea-going Robin Hoods. And who are you to say they're wrong?

Don't be insulting
Many of your friends might find your Jack Sparrow impression hilarious but it's doubtful whether your captors will. Not only have they seen it all before but they actually hate *Pirates of the Caribbean* (particularly number four, *On Stranger Tides*) and will fail to see any humour in your antics.

Don't undermine them
Don't attempt to convince the pirates that their mission is doomed and that a multinational coalition task force is on its way to rescue you and kill them. They've worked hard to make this mission a success, don't be a party pooper.

Be willing to discuss their ransom demands
Very few people have a price put on their head, but be prepared to put your case to the pirates if you feel the price they place on your survival is too low. If you think you're worth more than this, say for example, your family is extremely wealthy or you're a politically important hostage, then don't be afraid to say so. Your captors will thank you for bringing this to their attention.

Be aware of the Stockholm syndrome
Your abductors are aware of this notion, also known as traumatic bonding. After a few days they'll expect you to express sympathy for their cause and develop positive feelings towards them and their actions. Don't disappoint them.

48

Haggling when buying crystal meth

Once the accepted method of buying from a Moroccan carpet salesman or an Essex used-car dealer, the credit crisis has meant that haggling in business has become much more commonplace. Retailers in all walks of life are now willing to negotiate to make a sale; this includes crystal meth dealers, who have been hit by the recession as hard as anyone.

Despite the practice losing a lot of its stigma, more people are worried about the process of haggling than the actual fact they're buying Class-A narcotics in a darkened alley from a dangerous-looking stranger. Don't be. Drug dealers need your trade and as long as you abide by the following protocols, your meth deal should be quick, easy and at a price that's acceptable to both parties.

HOW TO HAGGLE FOR CRANK

Set your budget
The first question to ask yourself is 'How much do I want to spend to binge and crash?' Once you've set that figure your objective is to find the meth deal that offers the best value (purity vs quantity) for that sum of money.

Do your research
The next step is to research the meth you want to buy: rocks, pills, powder or liquid. Get an idea of current pricing by talking to other meth users and dealers (hookers can be another useful source of information). Knowing how much you can buy it for in the neighbourhood puts you in a strong bargaining position.

What to wear
Wearing expensive clothes will make the dealer think money is no object. However, if you're an meth addict, then turning up looking like a gaunt, toothless sleazeball gives the impression that you're so desperate for your fix you'll pay anything. The happy medium is smart casual.

Build a rapport with the dealer
Approach the dealer, smile and ask their name. It's highly unlikely that he/she will volunteer their real name but this doesn't matter. Whether they say they're called 'Mister White', 'the Ice Man' or 'Dr Feelgood', use it as many times as possible in conversation in order to build up a relationship. It's always best to precede any business with some light-hearted banter. If you're unsure what to discuss, just talk about the weather, football or the difference between Levo-methamphetamine and Dextro-methamphetamine.

Don't rush into negotiations

Avoid getting drawn into discussions about the price too soon. Let the dealer know you're interested but ask him/her about the meth. For example, is it pure or cut with powdered formula milk or talc? Is Yellow Bam better than Amber? Using the right lingo will show you're savvy to the crystal meth scene and relaxes them.

Talking numbers

Eventually the small talk will reach a natural conclusion and the time will come to get down and dirty on the price. Never tell the dealer what you've got to spend. The whole point of haggling is to avoid spending your maximum budget; wait for him/her to tell you his/her price for the meth.

Don't appear too keen

Acknowledge the price with a look of disappointment. Don't be insulting and shout something like, 'You've got to be fucking kidding me, man!' Both of you want to do the deal, so stay focused and positive. To get the best price for your meth you have to counter his/her price with a low offer to get a reaction. For example, if he/she is selling half a gram for £40, offer £18. There's no point in offering £35 as you'll never know how low he would have gone. Your objective at this point is to get a reaction like, 'You're out of your fucking mind, man. It costs me more than that from the lab!' while being thrown hard against a dumpster. That way you've established what's known as the basement price; now you can continue with the negotiations.

Offer and counter-offer

Make a counter-offer, say £24, nodding your head as you do so. This sends out a subtle, subliminal message to the dealer, but don't say anything else until he/she replies. Silence is strength in negotiations. If the dealer is interested in a sale he/she will make a counter-offer. Haggling can continue until you're happy with the price; precede your final offer by saying, 'If we can agree £x then I'm ready to buy'. If the dealer is adamant on his final offer then you still might be able to improve on it by asking for extras: 'OK, I'll buy two shards of crank but only if you throw in a quarter-gee of Donkey Dust.'

Clinching the deal
Only you can decide when to agree the deal. This will depend on how comfortable you are with the value, whether you think there's wriggle room on the price – and how desperate you are for a fix. Shake on a deal and make the payment in cash.

Know when to walk away
Don't feel pressured to buy and always be prepared to walk away from the deal. Remember that it's an addict's market; there's always someone in dodgy neighbourhoods and clubs willing to sell you poor man's cocaine.

CONCLUSION

Use what you've learned from haggling in your next meth deal. Remember, unlike taking crystal meth itself, the more you do it, the better you become.

49

Bailing out of a bad date with decency

Y ou're sitting across the restaurant table on a first date and the complete and utter lack of chemistry between you and your partner is palpable. You're not remotely attracted to them and from the small talk so far it's obvious that the only thing you have in common is that you have nothing in common. Your heart sinks as you realise that if you actually manage to stay awake it's going to be excruciatingly painful just getting past the bowl of pitted olives, let alone the appetiser.

Although it's tempting, getting up and walking out will be upsetting and traumatic for your date and likely to undermine any sense of their self-worth. In order to avoid being the cause of acute psychological scarring you have to find a rational excuse to bring the date to an early termination.

The reason of course doesn't need to be authentic. It just needs to sound genuine...

ACCEPTABLE WAYS TO BRING THE DATE TO AN EARLY CONCLUSION

Set an 'end time'
At the start of the date mention you have to be somewhere else at a pre-determined time. This isn't as easy as it sounds; the reason you give has to be one where your date will automatically realise he/she isn't welcome or doesn't want to be there, without you having to blatantly tell them that.

Bad examples
You: 'I'm meeting my friends at 9.30.'
Date: 'That sounds fun! I'd love to meet them too.'

You: 'I've got to pick my folks up from the airport.'
Date: 'Great! I love romantic drives on moonlit nights.'

Good examples
You: 'I have to check in with my parole officer at nine.'
Date: 'Oh.'

You: 'I need to break into the morgue at ten so I can fiddle with the cadavers.'
Date: 'I have to go now.'

Rescue by phone
Getting a friend to call you at a pre-determined time is a tried-and-tested method to extricate you from a bad date but avoid cliché excuses involving a friend in a car crash, a baby being born prematurely, your flatmate being locked out, a burst pipe or the sudden death of a parent or pet. (For advice, refer to the section 'Leaving a Party Early', p.107.)

Be 'on call'

Before the date takes place, lie about your job so that you have the perfect excuse to leave immediately, but be careful not to expose yourself as a pathological liar. For example, claiming you're the Prime Minister would give you enough of a reason to suddenly leave in the middle of the crispy fried duck, but what this job gives you in validity to bail early it lacks in credibility.

<u>Ten jobs where you'll be 'on call' 24/7</u>

1. Surgeon (or anyone else whose job involves being in an operating theatre)
2. Bomb disposal expert
3. Astronaut
4. Assassin
5. Secret agent
6. Siege negotiator
7. Anything at all to do with the air ambulance
8. Secretary-General of the United Nations
9. Exorcist
10. Miley Cyrus's publicist

<u>Ten jobs where it's highly unlikely you'll be 'on call' 24/7</u>

1. Chartered accountant
2. Milkman
3. Lap dancer
4. Lollipop lady
5. Anything at all to do with fast food
6. Nursery school teacher
7. The girl who holds up the round numbers in a boxing match

8. Crossword devisor
9. Turkey masturbator
10. Hairdresser

It's not me, it's you...
Getting your date to bring the evening to a close removes the
pressure on you to think of a reasonable and effective excuse.
In order to turn the tables on them, all you need to do is say or
do something that will make your date think you're dull, insane
or just plain creepy.

<u>Fifteen things to say or do to make sure it's your date's</u>
<u>decision to leave early</u>

1. Ask your date if they've ever been arrested. When they say,
   'No, have you?' smile and say, 'Yes, several times actually.
   Twice for attempted murder.'
2. Hand them a psychometric test and treat the whole date
   like a job interview.
3. Say that your hobby is eating paper serviettes and
   regurgitating them. Demonstrate.
4. Say that you're a pre-op transsexual.
5. Ask, 'Do you have a high tolerance to pain?'
6. Draw a swastika on your forehead and ask if they want to
   join your death cult.
7. Lean forward and whisper conspiratorially, 'I can't say too
   much but the Lizard Men are controlling me. Act normal.'
8. Say that you've just put a Wicca curse on them.
9. Recite pi to 200 places.
10. Order mashed potato, couscous or rice and start
    obsessively modelling The Devils Tower monument from
    Close Encounters of the Third Kind.

11. Laugh like a maniac and say, 'I wonder what your head looks like on a stick!'
12. Sing 'You've Lost That Loving Feeling' while making armpit farts.
13. Laugh raucously so that the entire content of your nose drops out.
14. Take fifty minutes to explain the intricacies of your job as a traffic light engineer.
15. Start a loud argument about breadsticks.

50

Pretending you're a rocket scientist to impress women

Desperate times call for desperate measures. You've been playing your best game but despite all your efforts, the sexy girl at the bar hasn't been at all impressed with your chat-up lines, your cheesy come-ons, your designer logos or your BMW key ring. It's almost time for last orders so you decide to go for broke.

'Did I tell you I'm a rocket scientist?'
On hearing this revelation she raises her eyebrows.
'I thought you just said you were a cage fighter.'
'Er... yes. But that's just a hobby, really. My 9–5 is a rocket scientist.'
She leans in towards you and you notice her pupils dilating.
'Really? That sounds interesting,' she purrs. 'Intelligent men really turn me on. What exactly do you do then?'
You gulp and begin to sweat. You have no absolutely no idea what the job entails, only that it involves rockets... and science.

Busted!

And like a wayward rocket, any hope that you'll be leaving the bar together comes crashing down to Earth.

If you're going to pretend you're a rocket scientist to get the girl (and let's face it, who hasn't?) then you have to follow through. In order to carry the charade off it's important to walk the walk *and* talk the talk…

HOW TO BE A CONVINCING ROCKET SCIENTIST

Attire
- White lab coat over a suit
- Anything worn by Dr Leonard Hofstadter from *The Big Bang Theory*

Accessories
- Glasses
- Pens in the breast pocket
- Slide rule
- *The Right Stuff* DVD
- Chart of the constellations

Buzzwords to use in conversation to show you're brainy
- The Tsiolkovsky rocket equation
- Orbital station keeping

Buzzwords to use in conversation to show you're brainy and naughty
- Thrust
- Re-entry

Questions you may be asked to ascertain if you're a credible rocket scientist	What to say	What not to say
So, what do you do exactly?	I devise and test avionics guidance control software	I make sure the pointy bit is at the top
What qualifications do you have?	Masters degree in aerospace engineering	Lots
Where do you work?	NASA	Moonbase Alpha
Who's your childhood hero?	Stephen Hawking	Steven Gerrard
What did you think of the film *Gravity*?	It was OK, but in reality the orbital planes of the Hubble Telescope, the International Space Station and the Chinese space station are not even co-aligned	Sandra Bullock? Phwoar!
What's your idea of a perfect date?	You and me walking along a moonlit beach, the warm water lapping at our feet, discussing the law of universal gravitation	You, me, a tub of apricot yoghurt and a sable glove

Questions you may be asked to ascertain if you're a credible rocket scientist	What to say	What not to say
What's the slogan on your favourite T-shirt?	'Gravity brings me down'	'Don't be sexist. The bitches hate it'
What do you think about The Big Bang Theory?	Do you mean the prevailing cosmological model for the early development of the universe or the popular TV series?	Say, what?
Tell me all about the night sky	It looks like someone took the stars from the heavens and put them in your eyes	There will only be seven planets left when I've finished pounding Uranus!
What's your favourite sexual postion?	1000101	69

51

Tipping a hooker

While tipping a hooker is not mandatory, prostitution is like any other service position. If you think the girl has done a good job, tip her accordingly. In some instances your ho will have already included a gratuity in her charges and while you can't be forced to tip, you are required to pay this extra amount as long as it's been clearly indicated beforehand. It's vital that you establish this before any sex act commences since any disputes that take place afterwards are likely to be settled not by a judge in a courtroom, but by her pimp in an alleyway.

TIPPING HOOKERS: Q & A

Is it best to tip the hooker directly?
Definitely. It's best to hand the tip directly to the girl you're rewarding. This prevents her pimp or the bordello owner skimming off a percentage.

I'm going to a brothel. Can I add the tip to my credit card?
Unless you absolutely need to charge the tip for business reasons, a cash tip is always better for the hooker.

Where do I put the tip?
Very few hookers use tip jars, so it's most common to leave the cash on the bedside table. If there's no bedside table (for example, you might be doing it on a dirty mattress on a crack house floor or against a dumpster round the back of a bar), then hand it to her personally.

Can I throw it at her?
No, the rule of thumb is treat your ho just like you would your waitress (well, except for asking her what the soup of the day is).

If I enjoy the service of two hookers do I have to tip them the same amount each?
No, the percentages shown opposite indicate the total gratuity. They will have to split the tip between them.

SUGGESTED TIP GUIDE – SEE OPPOSITE

Please note:
In many cases, a gratuity of 15 per cent will automatically be added for parties of eight or more.

Tip	Satisfaction Level	Possible Reasons
No tip	Extremely dissatisfied	She stole your wallet. She had crabs. Her crack dealer burst in, screamed at her, and totally ruined the ambience. She was born a man.
5 per cent	Dissatisfied	She hadn't shaved her legs. She sniggered when you undressed. She kept looking at her watch. She insisted on watching TV as you did it doggie-style. She played Candy Crush in the middle. She kept calling you 'Daddy'.
10 per cent	Satisfied	Her 'yes, yes, yes, yes, YES!' was extremely credible. She called you 'big boy' and you didn't detect any sense of irony in her voice. She didn't steal your watch.
15 per cent	Very satisfied	You got ten extra minutes FOC. She swallowed. She looked like Sandra Bullock.
20 per cent	Extremely satisfied	Her best friend joined in at no extra cost. She performed THAT act. She looked like a hot Sandra Bullock.

52

Meeting the parents

Meeting your girlfriend or boyfriend's parents for the first time is a significant stage in any relationship. You're moving on from casual dating to formalising the arrangement – showing your parents that you're serious about your partner and, unofficially, seeking their approval (or at least their tolerance).

The experience can be anything from nerve-racking to completely traumatic. You're in the spotlight and under pressure to come across as considerate, polite, loving, entertaining, charming and selfless. Even Nelson Mandela or Mother Teresa would have found it difficult to meet these expectations.

And that's why it's vital you don't say or do the wrong thing.

TWENTY-FIVE THINGS NOT TO SAY TO YOUR GIRLFRIEND'S PARENTS

1. And the funny thing is, we've been dating for about six months and my wife still doesn't have a clue!
2. My hobbies? Taxidermy and making snuff movies.

Remember, you don't get a second chance to make a first impression.

3. My father? He's in a mental institution. As was his father, and his father before him.

4. How did we meet? Well, she was my prison pen pal.

5. I'm sorry if I seem suicidal tonight. I'm in a very, very dark place.

6. Your daughter is safe with me, sir. I'm a Jedi Master and well versed in the Force.

7. How do you feel about a ménage à trois?

8. Ma'am, it looks like your face caught fire and someone tried to put it out with a fork.

9. Actually, it's probably more accurate to call me her 'boyfriend-slash-pimp'.

10. I just knew she was the girl for me when she told me about your large life insurance policy and your heart condition.

11. That reminds me of the time we thought the condom broke! (then nudge her father in the ribs.)

12. Am I religious? Well, I worship Lucifer. Does that count?

13. So, do you have a problem with polygamy?

14. My intentions? What do you mean? This is just for free sex.

15. Do you mind if I torch my car outside your house? It's stolen.

16. What I find touching is how you love nature despite what it's done to you.

17. Which one of you taught her to go down like that?

18. I love children… unfortunately that's why I ended up on the Sex Offenders Register.

19. Don't believe her story about how she got bruised. She walked into a door, all right?

20. Please to meet you, Ma'am. I can see who she got her tits from.

21. Any drug you want at street price less 10 per cent, just ask.

22. Hitler? No, I wouldn't say he was evil. Just misunderstood.
23. That's the great thing! No one has any idea I used to be a woman.
24. Favourite music? That's got to be Justin Bieber.
25. I see dead people.

TWENTY-FIVE THINGS NOT TO SAY TO YOUR BOYFRIEND'S PARENTS

1. I was so flattered when I found out he was a fan of my adult films.
2. Your décor and furniture… you're trying to be ironic, right?
3. He told you I was acting as a surrogate? That's soooo sweet! The truth is I got knocked up by my old boyfriend.
4. Sure I look familiar! I was all over the news a few years back after that bank hold-up.
5. Marriage? Of course I believe in it. I've done it four times before.
6. Siblings? Well, I have a brother. Well, brother-slash-lover, but it's OK. We're not dating any more.
7. My arm? I broke it when I slipped off the stripper's pole. Rookie mistake really.
8. See these nipple rings? Only had them done last week.
9. And the funny thing is, we both buy our Ecstasy tablets from the same dealer!
10. There's nothing that beats that great feeling of knowing your chlamydia test results are negative! I'm sure his will be OK too.
11. I can't wait until next year… Then I'll be old enough to drive.
12. I've heard so much about you… admittedly, hardly any of it good.

13. What a house! You must be loaded. To be honest, I wasn't sure how this relationship was going but this visit has totally made up my mind.

14. My life plan? Get married, contrive a divorce and take him to the fucking cleaners!

15. So, where do you stand on human sacrifice?

16. I really need a fix. Can you lend me some money?

17. What do I like best about him? That'll be his penis.

18. My parole officer says your son is a very calming influence on me.

19. I've been told my burps smell like farts.

20. I bet he's told you about my trick with the ping-pong ball.

21. A glass of wine? Why not? We can celebrate me coming out of rehab.

22. Ma'am, you've got something on your chin... No, the other one!

23. Is that a photo of the two of you? Wow, you used to be fairly attractive!

24. Did you hear the one about the Pope, the golden retriever and the dildo?

25. A boyfriend's father once tried to get to know me. I ate his liver with some fava beans and a nice Chianti.

53

How to behave at a swingers' party

If the idea of having consensual sex with unattractive people in badly decorated suburban homes appeals to you, then you'll be attracted to the 'swinging' scene, the practice formerly known as 'wife swapping'.

Swinging is one of those notions where the promise has far more appeal than the reality. Sure, in southern California the swinging scene involves tanned and toned athletic couples frolicking in hot tubs. In England, however, a swinging party is more likely to resemble a scene from the film *The Human Centipede* taking place in someone's damp conservatory.

If you're invited to a swingers' party you should behave exactly as you would if you were attending a normal party (well, apart from doing it doggie-style on the stairs halfway through the evening). Follow these rules and you should have an enjoyable time.

SWINGING DOS AND DON'TS

Do bring a gift
While it's not mandatory, a gift illustrates your appreciation at being invited. Don't be afraid to bring something relevant to the occasion: a bottle of lube is just as acceptable as supermarket own label Pinot Grigio. Suitable gifts also include condoms, chocolate body paint or a butt plug.

Do introduce yourself
Everyone at the party is there for the same reasons – sex and the buffet – so there's no need to be bashful. Just walk up to someone and introduce yourself just like you would if you met strangers anywhere else. For example, 'Hi, I'm _____ and this is my partner _____. She likes threesomes and I want to watch people pee.' If it's obvious that they don't really want to chat (or they're repulsed by your sexual preferences), just move away and introduce yourself to someone else.

Remember, strangers are merely friends you haven't had sex with yet.

Do make small talk
Not everyone wants to jump into bed right away, so be prepared to make small talk to get to know the person you want to have sex with. You're not looking to come across as the next Oscar Wilde, so it's OK to break the ice with something innocuous like, 'Nice wallpaper' or 'I just love what they've done with that stripper's pole in the shed'.

Don't interrupt people
Not only is it considered rude to try and start a conversation with someone if they're involved in an intimate sexual act,

it's sometimes also difficult for them to talk with their mouth full.

Don't be negative

For many people swinging is an escape from their tedious, lacklustre lives, so avoid saying anything that would compromise their enjoyment of the evening. Topics usually considered off-limits include STIs, premature ejaculation or crabs.

Don't touch without permission

If you want to touch someone, you need their consent. This applies to kissing, hugging, stroking, groping or prodding. You need to be clear in your intentions and understand that any permission granted may be for one time only. For example, a woman may let you lick her armpit but that doesn't mean you can automatically lick it again later that evening.

Do be polite

If you want to turn someone down, a polite 'No, thank you' is enough. If you feel you need to give a reason, all you have to say is, 'No thanks, you're not our/my type'. There's no need for you to explain *why* they're not your type (such as because you don't find stretch marks or obesity remotely sexually alluring).

Don't assume it's OK to join in

Just because you see someone inserting vegetables into a naked man's bottom don't think that it's OK for you to grab a courgette and just join in. Permission has to be sought and granted (see 'Don't touch without permission', above).

Don't cause a scene

If you have a problem as a couple, deal with it at home. Screaming at your partner, 'Yeah! Funny how you can suddenly find HER G-spot!' will quickly destroy the mood and can bring down a whole party.

Do respect your host's home

House rules are there to protect your host's home from damage so whether it's 'No more than three people in the bath at any one time' or 'No jizz on the sofa', make sure you understand the rules and abide by them.

Don't involve pets

Your hosts want their dogs and cats to remain innocent spectators and not collateral damage, so make sure any sexual acts do not involve (or rely on) the involvement of their pets. Remember: two legs good, four legs bad.

Don't be naked near the buffet

Finding a hair in your food is off-putting; finding a wayward pube is worse. Sex and the sandwiches, never the twain shall meet.

TEN WAYS TO RECOGNISE YOU'RE AT A SWINGERS' PARTY

1. You really look forward to not knowing anyone there.
2. Being called a slut is considered a term of endearment.
3. There's a mirror on the lounge wall… and the ceiling.
4. Someone is eating canapés off your wife's bare bottom.
5. Your selfies all have your head out of frame.
6. You come home with that *There's Something About Mary* hairstyle.
7. Your partner is having an orgasm while you're in another room.
8. A complete stranger asks you if you're allergic to latex.
9. Wearing a thong is considered being overdressed.
10. You're glad to go back to work so you can have a rest.

54

Knowing when to shake, kiss, hug or high-five

Welcome to Hello Hell – when you go in for a handshake but misread the situation and end up jabbing the other person's stomach as they lean in for a hug. Or you go in for a fist bump but they're ready for a high-five and you punch them in the wrist. Or worst still, you go in for the double air kiss but the person was expecting just one and turned their face away early. Your lips brush… and it's your sister.

It wasn't that long ago when a handshake was the default greeting for friends and business associates. Kisses were kept for loved ones and the only time men hugged was in bouts of Greco-Roman wrestling. Nowadays, it seems anything goes – and that's the problem. Adopting greetings from different cultures means there's now not only a huge variety to choose from, but because of the differences in people's expectations and boundaries there's are even more ways to behave inappropriately or look dorky.

To avoid embarrassment ensure you follow the Greetings Suitability Guide.

GREETINGS SUITABILITY GUIDE

Greeting	The only people permitted to perform this type of greeting
Handshake	Anyone
Handshake where you simultaneously wiggle your middle finger	Anyone wanting to come across as 'that creep'
Funny handshake	Freemasons
Handshake followed by a hug	Long-lost friends
High-five	Anyone under eighteen
Nose rubbing	Inuits
Fist bump	Homies, rappers
Peace out (thump chest twice then make peace sign)	Rock stars
Shoulder punch	Sportsmen, mates in the pub
The air kiss (also known as the 'social kiss')	Ladies who lunch
The double air kiss (also known as the 'mwah-mwah')	C-list celebrities
Kiss on the forehead	Mothers (on babies)
Kiss on the cheek	Close friends
Kiss on both cheeks	Anyone French

Greeting	The only people permitted to perform this type of greeting
Kiss on both cheeks, followed by a hug	Senior members of the Mafia
Kiss on the hand	Lecherous old men
Kiss on the lips	Lovers
Kiss on the ring	Anyone meeting the Pope
Kiss on the runway	Anyone who's travelled by Ryanair
Hug	Girls/young women Siblings Grandmas
Bear hug	Bears
Salute	Members of the Armed Forces
Nazi salute	Members of the Aryan Brotherhood
Vulcan salute	The cast of *Star Trek* films Anyone at a *Star Trek* convention
Smelling the cheek	Tuvalu islanders in the South Pacific Anyone wanting to be known forever as 'That fucking weirdo'

HOW TO AVOID MAKING A GREETINGS' MISTAKE

The group hug
Useful in a group dynamic, this method means you don't have to greet each person separately, thus avoiding the risk of getting it wrong multiple times.

Hold your arms wide apart, smile and say, 'You guys!' Walk forward and beckon them towards you, then embrace everyone in a group hug.

'I'm contagious'
Avoid any physical contact whatsoever by faking a contagious disease.

Cough loudly as you approach, saying, 'I wouldn't get too close, I've got a bad cold/the flu/green monkey disease/SARS/TB.'

If they persist, just before you reach them sneeze into your hands.

Keep your hands busy
Avoid any possibility of a physical greeting by making sure your hands are fully occupied. Examples include juggling, mixing a cocktail, squeezing a spot.

Go on the offensive
Put them on the back foot by inventing a new physical greeting. This will catch them off-guard and they'll panic – with the result that they'll be the ones doing something inappropriate, not you. Suggestions include: brisk clapping, waving furiously with both hands, knocking elbows or pressing foreheads.

55

Flat sharing with a gorilla

While having a 204kg (450lb) silverback gorilla as a housemate will give you a certain degree of security, and their height and arm length are useful for replacing light bulbs, don't expect the same fun and high-jinx as in an episode of *Friends*. They sleep for thirteen hours a day and can be quite lazy, relying on their threatening reputation of having the strength of four to six men to avoid pulling their weight or accepting responsibility.

The key to avoiding conflict is to establish ground rules from the start. A formal agreement between you and the gorilla makes the financial obligations of each party clear as well as establishing chore-sharing duties and what constitutes acceptable behaviour.

Although essential in setting guidelines and boundaries, it's important to know that Gorilla Co-Tenancy agreements are not usually legally binding (mainly because gorillas can't read or write, and are just as likely to eat the agreement than abide by it).

Since gorillas have opposable thumbs, there is no excuse for them not to take part in vacuuming, dusting and cleaning duties.

SAMPLE GORILLA CO-TENANCY AGREEMENT

Rule 1: My bedroom is off limits
Foraging should take place outside the flat, not in my bedroom. The only food you'll find here is a packet of Wrigley's Doublemint on top of my dressing table so don't bother looking!

Rule 2: Don't throw faeces
Do I really need to elaborate?

Rule 3: No overnight guests
I have no problem with any of your mates or children visiting but having 6–12 lowland gorillas staying in my flat is not only impractical and unhygienic, it also breaks the terms of my lease.

Rule 4: Clear up your mess
If you make a mess, clean it up. This applies to litter, crumbs, shed hair or piles of steaming faeces (*see also* Rule 5).

Rule 5: Keep the bathroom clean
The toilet is a fundamental bathroom fixture, not a decoration so please use it. If you block the toilet (highly likely, given your high-fibre diet) then use the plunger to unclog it; do NOT leave it for me to do. I have a busy and stressful job and the last thing I want to do when I get home is clear gorilla excrement out of the toilet or from the walls, ceilings or floor.

Rule 6: Don't borrow my clothes without asking
We may be closely related in DNA terms, but don't assume you can borrow my clothes, particularly shoes and designer tops. If I do give permission for you to borrow any item of clothing and

you spill something on it (like gorilla drool), you are responsible for having it professionally cleaned or replaced.

Rule 7: Don't leave banana skins on the floor
Not only is this untidy and unsanitary, it also constitutes a health hazard (*see also* Rule 4).

Rule 8: You call, you pay
Local calls are free, but you are responsible for any long-distance calls made to your family in Gabon, Angola or the Democratic Republic of Congo.

Rule 9: Don't take my food
I know you eat up to 27kg (60lb) of vegetation a day but funnily enough I also like fresh fruit, so when two bags of Conference pears or Gala apples suddenly appear in the fruit bowl, don't automatically assume that half of it is yours.

Rule 10: Respect the fridge
Your two shelves are the lower two, so please restrict your food storage to this area and the right-hand salad bin. I know the fridge light is fascinating to you but after you've opened and closed the door twenty times to figure out what's going on, make sure it's left shut.

Rule 11: Be mindful of our neighbours
Chest beating, grunting, and roaring 'George, George, George of the Jungle' should be kept to a minimum before 7am (9am at weekends) and after 10pm.

Rule 12: Television time
The large flatscreen TV in the lounge shall be shared; however,

live TV viewing shall take priority over watching DVDs (there's only so many times I can bear to watch *King Kong*, *Mighty Joe Young*, *Battle for the Planet of the Apes* and documentaries about Dian Fossey).

Rule 13: Don't use my razor under any circumstances

Not only is this extremely unhygienic but your fur will blunt all five blades of my Venus Breeze within moments, severely compromising its ability to 'reveal the goddess in me'.

Rule 14: Chores

I realise that when you're not sleeping, you're looking for food and when you're not looking for food, you're resting, however sufficient time has to be set aside each weekend for household chores. Since you have opposable thumbs on both your hands and feet there is no excuse for you not to take part in vacuuming, dusting and cleaning duties.

Rule 15: Hands off my plants

I appreciate that gorillas have been known to eat over 200 species of vegetation but my yucca in the living room is not one of them, OK?

Rule 16: Respect the need for 'me time'

If you see me sitting on the sofa reading a book or using my iPad, don't try and interrupt me or play with my hair, looking for bugs to eat.

Rule 17: Resolving disputes

Any disagreements will be settled by the use of a mediator, not by brute force.

56

How to help a
Sudoku addict

It usually starts as an impulse buy at an airport or railway station bookshop. It looks innocuous enough, just a collection of nine 3x3 grids containing a selection of random numbers. You've seen people play Sudoku on your daily commute but you've always scoffed at the idea. An utter waste of time, a stupid number puzzle for losers... Now, faced with a long journey, you decide to give it a go to while away the time. 'How hard can this be?' you ask yourself as you turn to the first puzzle. Two hours later and BAM! – you're hooked.

Sweating with excitement and anticipation, you rush to the nearest bookshop and buy another Sudoku book. Then another... then three more. In less than a month you've progressed from puzzle ratings 'easy' to 'extreme'. Then someone sees you working on a puzzle and furtively tells you that he knows of an online site called Samurai Sudoku with overlapping grids that's compatible with all browsers... Suddenly your family, friends and work colleagues don't really exist: there is only Sudoku. That's when you know you're a Sudokuholic.

Sounds familiar?

Many people know someone who's addicted to Sudoku. It's a puzzle that crosses gender, age, class and race. There are many misconceptions about how to help such an addict. Some people think it's easy to muster up enough willpower to give up the grid but the truth is that Sudoku addiction is a complex form of mental illness and conquering it is a hard-fought battle. That said, if help comes early enough – and by following the steps below – it is possible to help someone overcome Sudoku dependency and return to a normal, square-free life.

Step 1

RECOGNISE THAT YOUR FRIEND OR LOVED ONE MIGHT HAVE A SUDOKU PROBLEM
- Has he/she undergone a marked personality change? Difficult puzzles can make individuals feel isolated, helpless or angry.
- When you recently walked with them past a hopscotch grid did they say they felt weirdly giddy?
- Have they admitted money problems? Many Sudoku addicts resort to selling off prized possessions or turning to theft in order to fund their need for puzzle books and pens.
- Ink stains may be evident on the fingers and hands of a Sudoku addict, although many become skilled at hiding evidence of their dependency by wearing gloves.
- Has there been a sudden change in their behaviour – for example, euphoria, irritability, anxiety and muttering the numbers one to nine under their breath?

• Has his/her behaviour become more secretive or suspicious
  – for example, after being online all day behind closed doors
  do they always delete their Google history?

Step 2

CONSIDER STAGING AN INTERVENTION

This is a way of showing the Sudoku addict that his/her loved
ones have also been affected by the problem and that they care
enough to want to help. Begin by explaining the problem
and the consequences and conclude by proposing an effective
treatment (see Step 3, below).

Note: The intervention should be positive; it's not an excuse to
punish, threaten, preach or rip up their Sudoku books in front
of them.

Step 3

ENROL THE ADDICT IN AN APPROPRIATE
SUDOKU REHABILITATION PROGRAMME

There are a number of different Sudoku rehab clinics offering
a variety of programmes. The traditional method is to wean
the addict off Sudoku and on to other, softer puzzles under
controlled conditions, such as word searches or logic problems.
Other therapies gradually replace Sudoku with crosswords
or Scrabble, while one pioneering clinic uses a controversial
approach involving Angry Birds.

Step 4

BE SUPPORTIVE THROUGHOUT

With any form of rehabilitation, relapses are common. Your friend shouldn't see this as a failure but an inevitable step in his/her recovery. You need to be there and offer support on their long, numberless journey to becoming a Sudoku survivor.

Step 5

ENCOURAGE HEALTHIER PUZZLES AFTER RECOVERY

Introduce your friend to a new range of pastimes that are just as strategic but a lot less addictive; games that are not solo activities. Success has been achieved by the introduction of chess, dominos, cribbage, backgammon and mahjong (but avoid Candy Crush Saga at all costs).

57

How to be a good prison bitch

If you're unfortunate/deserving enough to end up in prison it's important to know that like most institutions, there's a clearly defined hierarchy. The prison class system isn't written down, nor is it spoken about, it just is.

The more glamorous the crime, the higher up the social ladder you are. At the top are serial killers, closely followed by murderers and armed robbers; in the middle are those in for fraud, embezzlement or petty theft, while at the bottom are those in for various sex crimes. However, there's a level below even that of nonce – and that's the prison bitch. If you do find yourself in this unenviable position be prepared to lose any sense of dignity, self-worth – and your ability to sit down without wincing. To fulfil your obligations as a prison bitch it's important to understand the responsibilities associated with the position.

FAQS ABOUT PRISON BITCHES

Is a prison bitch the same as being another convict's PA?
Yes, as long as you substitute the word 'PA' for 'Sex Slave'.

How do I become a prison bitch?
Be weak, shy or scared, or suffer from incredible low self-esteem.

What is the key to a successful prison bitch/cellmate relationship?
Respect (and the ability to stifle tears and cries of pain after lights out).

What are my responsibilities as a prison bitch?
• Being submissive
• Having an intimate yet degrading relationship with your cellmate.
• Going by the name of 'wifey'.
• Getting abused and beaten up regularly by Big Bubba.
• Being pimped out to other inmates in return for smokes, tinned apricots or a chocolate bar.

What are the benefits?
• Being protected by your cellmate.
• That's about it…

HOW TO TURN YOUR CELLMATE INTO A SOULMATE

Keep the cell neat and tidy
Whether he's in the exercise yard or starting a riot, your cellmate will be absent a lot of the time, giving you the perfect

opportunity to tidy the cell. Gather up old newspapers and clothes, plump up the pillows to remove those bite marks, run a duster over the bunks and bars and ensure the washbasin and toilet bowl are sparkling. It's important that when your cellmate returns he feels like he's entered a sanctuary rather than a cell, and his satisfaction will give you a lift too.

Don't burden him with complaints and problems

You might have been abused in the library by that psycho from Block E or your tattoo made with a pin and biro ink may have gone septic but whatever happened and no matter how bad your day, keep these thoughts to yourself. Your cellmate's probably had a hard day himself on the chain gang so don't offload your problems as soon as he walks back in.

Give him space

Never complain if he comes back from the mess hall late or goes to the secret card game with the guards without you. Instead try to understand the pressures he's under serving his twenty-year stretch and the very real need to have 'me time' once in a while.

Keep up your appearance

You want to look your best for your cellmate, so make sure you're presentable at all times. Style your hair, use deodorant and make sure your prison uniform is crisp and clean. Accessorise it with a bangle made from half a handcuff or a belt created from a torn sheet worn low on the hips. Hoops cut from old toilet rolls make great earrings, while a combination of ink and gravy makes for effective mascara. Sometimes these small things make a big difference and your cellmate will appreciate you taking the trouble.

Be a good listener

Let him tell you his troubles — that lousy con who still owes him two ounces of coffee and five smokes, that sadistic guard who needs to be taught a lesson, the escape plan that's hit a snag… Your issues will seem trivial in comparison. Remember, one of your most important tasks is to build up and maintain his ego, which will get bruised as often as you do.

It's him, him, him… Not me, me, me…

Your cellmate comes first in all senses of the word. Be subservient and obedient at all times and respect his point of view. If you want something, like another tub of butter smuggled out of the kitchens or a new ribbon for your hair, just ask once. Anything more constitutes nagging, and nagging constitutes a beating.

Don't question his judgement

Never criticise your cellmate's actions or question his decisions — for example, asking, 'Is that shiv sharp enough?' or 'Do you have to pimp me out tonight?' Being incarcerated for twenty years (plus the fact he weighs 250lb and killed two people) means he's absolute master of the cell.

Remember, you're his bitch, not his wife

He might disappear from the cell one evening without telling you where he's gone, but you know he's turning that new fish in the laundry room. Recognise that a prison bitch mustn't get possessive or jealous. It's your duty to turn the other cheek and let him have some extra fun every now and then. Remember, when this happens it doesn't mean that he's stopped loving you.

58

Suspecting your husband is a Mafia don

Y ou're proud of your husband. Ever since you've known him he's worked hard to climb the greasy corporate pole. Now he's risen through the ranks to become head of a large multinational business and the whole family's benefiting from a lavish lifestyle. It's only when you stand back and think about it that you realise you're not actually sure what his company does. Sure, he talks about 'contracts' a lot of the time but the most he ever says about the organisation itself is that it has 'fingers in lots of pies'.

His reluctance to say more intrigues you, especially when you think about the way he does business. In his leadership position you'd expect him to use buzzwords like 'paradigm shift', 'synergy' or 'monetise'; instead all he seems to talk about is 'hits', 'stoolies' and 'bagmen'.

Even when he's not working there's something that doesn't quite add up. Most of his friends seem to be called Vinny, Nick or Dutch. And each time he takes you to a fancy restaurant, why is it you get to your table through the kitchen? That's when you suddenly realise that rather than being a CEO, he's actually a Mafia don. However, before you confront him about his secret (yet extremely lucrative) life, you need to make absolutely sure.

Step 1

CONSIDER THE EVIDENCE

Twelve signs your husband might work for the Mob and not a large corporation

1. He didn't get promoted, he got 'made'.
2. He refers to the various business operations as 'rackets'.
3. His board of directors all have nicknames such as Alphonse 'The Blade' Bartolo or Lou 'The Animal' Polizzi.
4. When he uses the term 'hostile takeover' he makes a cutting sign in front of his throat.
5. You heard him arguing with his finance director about whether a horse's head is tax deductible.
6. Also, you heard him say, 'Who the hell needs a non-disclosure agreement when we've got the omertà?'
7. Instead of a chairman he has a 'capo di tutti capi'.
8. Board meetings sometimes take place in meat lockers.
9. He calls employees 'wiseguys' and he's not being sarcastic.
10. The graduate trainee programme covers gambling, prostitution and extortion.
11. Yearly appraisals take into account the number of people whacked.
12. He told one of his staff to 'Leave the gun, take the cannoli' and he wasn't joking around.

Step 2

HOW TO REACT

If you recognise most of the signs above then it's highly likely your husband *is* a Mafia don. Don't worry, though. Being head of an organised crime syndicate isn't all bad. It might not be a conventional career but it's a job that engenders great respect, not only from his employees but also public officials like the mayor, local politicians and the chief of police. The perks include a very handsome remuneration and the ability to exert an enormous amount of power without any unwelcome interference from HR (why bother with a written warning when you get to make someone sleep with the fishes?).

And as long as you're happy being kept in a lifestyle that affords you a huge house, luxury cars, expensive clothes, lavish holidays and a generous amount of spending money it's best to keep quiet about it.

That way you'll have something else in common with your husband: your own code of silence.

59

Coping with stalkers

In most cases, it's good to be popular and the centre of attention. One instance when it's not is when someone tells you how much they love you while carrying chloroform and a roll of duct tape. This should be taken as a clue that instead of an admirer you've got yourself a stalker.

At first it's flattering that a random stranger likes you so much, but this can turn to worry when the stranger has the word GOD drawn on their forehead and your face tattooed on their back.

Stalkers come in many shapes and forms. Some are socially inept, some are just attention-seekers, while others are ruthless paranoid psychopaths with a basement and a thorough knowledge of knots. Regardless of whether their behaviour is annoying, comical or involves unpredictable violence, there are two main reasons why people stalk: they think you're their ideal partner or they want to punish you after being rejected as your ideal partner.

Once you've established you might have a stalker, follow the steps below to stay alive.

Sometimes there can be a fine line between having an admirer and having a stalker.

SHOULD I CONFRONT OR IGNORE A STALKER?

The best advice, as far as possible, is to not acknowledge their existence or respond to any communication. However, being ignored is likely to cause your stalker to get more angry and frustrated and even more intent on getting to you.

This is known as the Catch-22 of dealing with stalkers... Meh.

TWELVE SIGNS THAT SOMEONE IS STALKING YOU

1. They change their name to yours and dress exactly the same.
2. At 2am they phone you and say in a scary voice, 'I miss your musk'.
3. They carry a list of baby names for your future children together.
4. At midnight they show up at your home dressed up as Heath Ledger's Joker from *The Dark Knight*.
5. They send you a badly Photoshopped picture of you both as bride and groom.
6. They wait outside your house in their car and on the passenger seat are love letters and a loaded handgun.
7. They bombard you with upward of 200 emails a day (more than you get from that Nigerian Prince or the lovelorn Russian women).
8. They send you messages on Facebook like, 'I am going to find you and kill you and cut your head off, and put it on a stick and then wear your skin like a suit'. Then they get even more irritated when you don't click 'Like'.

9. They send you locks of their hair… and it's not from their head.
10. They refer to you as their 'prey'.
11. They say they plan to win your love by assassinating the President.
12. They have a collection of photos of you asleep.

HOW TO DEAL WITH IT

Step 1
Identify the stalker
Is he/she a friend or a relative, that odd-looking guy that works in Goods Inwards or just a random person? Your relationship with the stalker could be the difference between a few uncomfortable feelings or being tortured and left for dead in an abandoned house. For example, a friend is less likely to hurt you than a complete stranger (unless it's a friend who hears voices and collects knives).

Step 2
If it's a stranger, get a good description of the stalker
Take a note of their gender, skin colour, height, weight, hair and eye colour and clothing. The more information you can give the authorities, the better. For example, a bad description would be 'A tall man'. A good description would be 'A thin, wiry and balding man, about 6 feet 2 inches tall, with pockmarked, rodent features and the cold grey soulless eyes of a maniacal killer'.

Step 3
Inform somebody you're being stalked
Who you tell depends on who the stalker is. For example, if it's your dad, tell your mum. If it's someone from work, tell your line manager. If it's your line manager, tell your department head. And if it's a complete stranger, tell the police. If it's a celebrity, tell the media. It doesn't matter who you tell, as long as you tell someone, otherwise things could get worse (and by worse we mean anything from receiving nuisance phone calls day and night, to being abducted and eaten).

Step 4
Minimise your contact with the stalker
Until the authorities can take action, you need to minimise the chances of your stalker seeing or interacting with you. For example, don't use any social media sites, or if you're out and about and you see them, take a different route from usual or seek sanctuary in a public place. If practical, stay with a friend or close relative for a few days (unless, of course, that friend or close relative is the one with the collection of photos of you asleep).

60

Spontaneously combusting during a job interview

It's natural to feel worried before a big job interview. There's usually a lot riding on it – a change in your routine, better prospects, a much better salary and bonus package... Then there's the company car... And here you are sitting in front of a complete stranger who's scrutinising not just your CV but your appearance, mannerisms and what you have to say. No wonder you're feeling stressed out.

Anxiety and nervousness can manifest themselves in a number of ways: stomach cramps, babbling your answers, having your mind go blank, fidgeting and, of course, sweating. In some cases extreme stress can actually cause your body to spontaneously combust and although these instances are thankfully quite rare, it's important to know how to deal with this awkward and sometimes highly dangerous situation.

JOBS TO AVOID

If you are susceptible to Spontaneous Human Combustion (SHC) then it's probably best not to apply for these positions:

- Petrol-tanker driver
- Oil-rig engineer
- Bomb-disposal expert
- Solvent tester
- Anything at all to do with fireworks

WHAT TO DO

Don't admit that you may suffer from SHC
In a recent survey, 86 per cent of managers within 50 of the top FTSE 100 companies said they would not employ a candidate with a history of spontaneously bursting into flames. While this may be seen as discrimination it's advisable not to bring up the problem and risk prejudicing your chances.

Where practical, sit away from anything flammable
Many interviews take place in meeting rooms or conference rooms where the opportunity for fire damage is thankfully usually limited to cheap carpeting and furniture. If the interview takes place in someone's office try to sit as far away as possible from any paperwork or sophisticated and expensive computer equipment.

Don't let your proclivity to SHC affect your performance
Rehearse your answers to cliché questions so you're not caught off-guard and respond with an inappropriate answer. For example:

What do you see yourself doing in five years?
Good: Using the experience I've gained here to expand my skillset to become a department head.
Bad: Not bursting into flames.

Practice relaxation techniques
If you feel yourself getting hotter and hotter try and visualise something calming. Examples include someone extinguishing a fire in the middle of a field of beautiful wild flowers or extinguishing a fire on a sun-kissed tropical beach.

If you can't stop yourself from bursting into flames...
Assess the nature of the fire. Ask yourself 'Is it me?'
If the answer's 'yes', take these three actions to extinguish the flames:
– Stop*
– Drop
– Roll
* In most cases, the fact you've burst into flames will usually bring the interview to an end.

Try and rescue the situation
Although SHC can often count against you in an interview there is still a way to salvage the opportunity, and that's with a witty comeback to win over the interviewer. Examples include:

- 'What's that burning? That must be my ambition.'
- 'Come on, I must be the hottest prospect!'
- 'Don't stop the interview now, I'm on fire!'
- 'You know what they say… "Build a man a fire, and he'll be warm for a day. Set a man on fire, and he'll be warm for the rest of his life".'

Note: If you spontaneously combust and there's a fire extinguisher handy, use it. Don't worry about whether it's the right kind of extinguisher; it's unlikely that you'll make things worse.

61

Calling your wedding off

Whatever the reason for calling off your wedding, the emotional trauma is likely to take on the same characteristics: humiliation, embarrassment, rejection, awkwardness, sadness, loneliness, depression, fury and suicidal tendencies. Your natural instinct might be to sit in a corner of a room with your hands clutched around your knees, gently rocking back and forth, whimpering – but you have responsibilities.

Like all things connected to weddings there are procedures involved relating to who to tell, what to say and what to do. The good thing is that no matter how dejected and miserable you feel, you're not alone; a close friend (preferably one who's not smug or judgemental) can contact the guests and help you get through this very difficult time.

WHAT TO DO WHEN 'I DO' BECOMES 'I DON'T'

Let everyone on the guest list know at the earliest opportunity

To save face it's tempting to just say the wedding is postponed. However, friends and family might continue to make travel plans, hotel reservations or buy gifts – and pester you for the new date. If you definitely know the wedding is off then make sure all the guests know. The order of notification should be:

1. Your bezzie
2. Your ex-fiancé/fiancée
3. Everyone else

Make it official

The cancellation of the wedding should be as formal as the original wedding announcement itself. If parents organised the event, they should send a printed notification to every invitee. The reason for the cancellation can be given or left vague; either approach is acceptable.

Mr and Mrs Julian Clarke announce that the
wedding of their daughter Claire Clarke
and Mr Elliot Jackson
has been ended by mutual consent
and they hope he burns in Hell

Mr and Mrs James Leonard Regret that owing
to their future daughter-in-law
Having sex with the best man at the rehearsal dinner
They are obligated to recall the invitations
To the marriage reception of their son Ian
To his dirty whore slut fiancée Susan

MR AND MRS KEITH DAVISON ARE RELIEVED
TO ANNOUNCE THE CANCELLATION
OF THE WEDDING OF THEIR DAUGHTER
ANDREA TO MR RYAN JOHNSON
DUE TO THE FACT THAT SHE'S FOUND OUT SHE'S NOT
REALLY PREGNANT AFTER ALL

Return the gifts

The bread maker that won't even be removed from its box, the tacky gold-rimmed champagne flutes, the cheap-looking salad bowl and matching servers... It's good practice to return the gifts to the people who bought them – and see how they like receiving shit presents.

Negotiate the ring

This is a grey area. Under the law, an engagement ring is considered a gift; however, most courts consider it a 'conditional gift', i.e. its gift status is conditional on the wedding going ahead. Dealing with foul slimeball lawyers is often more distressing and painful than coping with a cancelled wedding, so it's best to abide by the accepted etiquette: if the woman broke the wedding off, she returns the ring; if it was the man, she keeps it. Simple.

Don't try and salvage the day
It's tempting to try and put a positive spin on events by changing the reception into a sort of 'Pre Wedding Divorce' party.

Don't.

After a wedding is cancelled you'll probably be left with very little dignity. Don't lose it all.

FIVE SIGNS IT MIGHT BE BEST TO CALL OFF YOUR WEDDING

For Him
1. She's already chosen your children's names, your friends, and your clothes.
2. She crumples your love poem into a ball and yells, 'I want a new pair of Jimmy Choos, not this shit!'
3. She sold her engagement ring to fund her next fix.
4. She tells you her hen weekend will involve her and her ex-boyfriend in Paris.
5. Her pet name for you is 'Sugar Daddy' not 'Honey Bunny'.

For Her
1. He says the word 'but' after 'I love you'.
2. He has sex four times a week… Twice as often as you.
3. He wants you to join his Holy War.
4. Whenever you talk about your future he says, 'meh'.
5. He wants a *Star Wars* themed-wedding… him as Han Solo and you as Chewbacca.

62

Writing
love letters

In this age of texts, tweets and rushed emails, a good old fashioned love letter is a lost art. It sounds easy enough; after all, how difficult can it be to put your heartfelt emotions down on paper? But there's an enormous skill in turning your feelings into words. A great love letter should hasten the recipient's heart rate and even move them to tears as they read and re-read every one of your well-chosen and genuinely loving sentiments.

It's often said that the difference between a good love letter and a bad one is whether it's kept or burned. To keep your beloved from reaching for the matches follow this advice.

THE DOS AND DON'TS OF LOVE LETTER WRITING

Do write your love letter by hand
This shows you care.

It's difficult to convey affection if your love letter resembles a kidnapping demand.

Don't cut out letters from a newspaper
This shows you're some sort of psychopath.

Don't send a photocopy
This will kill any romance stone-dead.

Don't make it too formal
Avoid phrases like 'To whom it may concern' and 'Dear Sir or Madam'.

Do say what you mean
A love letter should express your genuine devotion, desire and passion. It's a place to open your heart and pour out your true feelings, not a place to be bitingly ironic.

Trust the postal service
Just send it first class. Making your beloved get out of bed early to sign for your letter will be inconducive to putting them in a romantic frame of mind, while sending it by courier just makes you appear profligate and needy.

Do include a photograph
A small passport-size photo of you clipped to the letter is a nice personal touch. This allows your beloved to reflect on you with fondness while they read your sentiments. Sticking your head onto a photo of a porno model's body is not romantic; sticking your head onto a photo of your pet is just plain weird.

Do spray the letter with scent
Like including a photo, a little spritz of your aftershave or perfume will evoke a more emotive response. However, avoid dusting the letter with scented talc. Any leakage in transit will

make it look less like a thoughtful gesture and more like a terrorist anthrax attack.

Don't turn desire into desperation
It's fine to say how you feel 'whole' when you're with your beloved but saying that you cry or self-harm every minute you're apart just makes you sound desperate... Or mentally unstable.

Don't be afraid to use poetry
Including an extract from a love poem will make you appear thoughtful and sensitive, but choose your quotes carefully. The Romantic poets are generally accepted as being Keats, Shelley, Byron, Wordsworth and Coleridge. Eminem lyrics, while sometimes described as the 'poetry of the streets', are not recommended.

Do talk about the things you love most and admire about them
Good things to write about your beloved might include their innocence, their loyalty to their friends or their boundless optimism. The following attributes are probably not worth committing to paper: their trust fund, their low resistance to alcohol, or their tits.

Choose your analogies carefully
These should be evocative and dreamy. For example, 'Your eyes are like two diaphanous blue pools of crystalline clarity' and NOT 'Your eyes remind me of your really hot best friend'.

Don't expect them to write back right away
In many cases you'll get a quick acknowledgement saying how much the recipient was touched and how they love you even

more, but don't be disappointed if you don't hear back right away. Your beloved might be busy or feel awkward – or they may need to take time to compose a suitably romantic reply. Don't end your love letter with something you think is humorous but might come across as vaguely threatening ('Write back or I'll cut you').

Some people find background music helps them get in the mood for composing a romantic message that speaks right from the heart. Suggestions include 'You're The First, The Last, My Everything' by Barry White, or 'Eternal Flame' by The Bangles. Avoid 'I Hate Everything About You' by Three Days Grace or 'Pulse of the Maggots' by Slipknot.

63

Urinal etiquette

Unzip.
Go.
Shake.
Zip.
Wash hands.
Leave.

It sounds simple, doesn't it?

Any women reading this section might find it surprising that there even exists a need for any form of bathroom etiquette for men. The truth is that male toilet procedure is far more complicated than it seems. Where to stand, where to look, what to do with your hands... there are so many ways to get it wrong. Rules have existed as long as urinals have; it's just that they've been unwritten... until now.

The following guidelines have been carefully designed to make urinal use free from uncertainty, embarrassment – and, most importantly of all, confrontation.

THE URINAL 10 COMMANDMENTS

1. Thou shalt respect personal space at all times
When you first take your place at the urinal ensure there's at least one empty space between you and the next man. If there's no free space, loiter near the washbasin until a gap becomes available. If you only follow one rule for urinal use, make sure it's this one.

2. Thou shalt not make musical accompaniment
Singing, whistling, beat boxing, yodelling... no vocal accompaniment is permitted under any circumstances (particularly Mongolian throat singing). Not even if it's relevant or ironic — for example, humming 'Drip Drop' by Vanessa Hudgens or 'Can I Go' by Aslyn.

3. Thou shall not use thy smartphone
While the ability to simultaneously hold and manipulate different objects in each hand is admirable, the men's toilet is not the place. Not only is it unhygienic, it's highly unlikely that your piss is so important that you have to tweet about it.

4. Thou shalt not converse
Remember, you're standing in a toilet and not a pub, locker room or country club. There is absolutely no need to acknowledge your neighbour. However, if you are feeling exceptionally sociable, your greeting should be limited to a cursory nod or at most, a muffled, 'Alright?'

5. Thou shalt not touch
Unless you want to spend an evening in a police cell or A&E there is only person you are permitted to touch, and that's

yourself. Even accidentally brushing elbows can sometimes be mistaken for an inflammatory gesture or a wanton come-on.

6. Thou shalt not overdo the shake

The shake should be limited to two or three subtle flicks or jiggles. To judge the right sort of movement, imagine your penis is a spoon holding Parmesan cheese and the urinal is a bowl of minestrone. Remember, you're getting rid of excess urine, not wrestling with a fire hose.

7. Thou shalt not sneak a peek

While urinating either look straight ahead or up at the ceiling, as if contemplating your own existence. It's a good rule of thumb to remember that some degree of violence is likely to occur if you glance at any other man while holding your own penis.

8. Thou shalt always use at least one hand

'Hands free' should only ever be associated with mobile phones and driving. When urinating always use one or both hands. Standing there with your hands on your hips or behind your head is just showing off.

9. Thou shalt admit defeat early on

If you find yourself suffering from stage fright and realise that it may be several minutes before you can urinate, acknowledge the problem as soon as possible. Standing in front of a urinal while you concentrate for several minutes on the Trevi Fountain or Niagara Falls is just selfish.

10. Thou shalt wash thy hands

While urine itself is sterile, bacteria can still be present in any urinary tract infections so washing your hands is essential.

Note: The rabies virus can also be present in urine, although if you're infected with this, you've probably got more to worry about than making sure your hands are clean.

64

Composing a 'Dear John' letter

Crying, screaming, stamping up and down or the holding of breath… Emotions can run high when you tell someone face-to-face that your relationship is over. That's why a 'Dear John' or 'Dear Jane' letter is the better option. It gives you the opportunity to say goodbye without worrying about feeling cruel or getting angry – or worse still, entering into a conversation and being talked out of your decision.

The most common advice given for writing 'Dear John' letters is to be kind and sensitive, and avoid attacking the other person. It's also said that what you say in your letter should lead to positive change, helping your partner recognise his or her character flaws. Wrong!

A 'Dear John' letter should tell it how it is, warts and all… Especially if it concerns warts (and particularly if they're the genital ones). The worst thing you can do is pussyfoot around the reasons for your break-up so that the recipient believes he/ she has a second chance.

Your letter is not about a break, a sojourn or a sabbatical. It's not an ultimatum or even an apology.

Using the strongest language and sentiments, your 'Dear John' letter has to leave the recipient in absolutely no doubt that your relationship has been categorically, positively and undeniably terminated.

Or, as they say... Game over.

TEMPLATE FOR A 'DEAR JOHN'/'DEAR JANE' LETTER
Copy and choose from the appropriate options:

Dear [NAME],

I've been thinking long and hard about our relationship and quite frankly, dating you makes me feel _____

Choose from:
* nauseous
* trapped
* threatened
* suicidal
* disgusted that I'm seen out with you
* wretched
* full of hatred and self-loathing
* like a loser
* soiled

I admit that when we first met, I was in love with you. However, now that I've had time to relect on our time together I realise that far from being my soulmate, you are actually _____

Choose from:
- my biological brother/sister
- an epic douchebag
- a pretentious egomaniac
- a twisted psychopath
- a degenerate weirdo
- an emotional cripple
- a sadistic barbarian
- a borderline paedo
- an attention-seeking control freak
- a brutal fascist dictator
- frigid and distant
- the person most likely to appear on *Embarrassing Bodies*
- Adolf Hitler's clone

You're so insensitive and selfish you probably didn't even realise that for the last few months I've been _____

Choose from:
- unhappy
- drunk
- in denial
- praying for your death
- treated like a chump
- taken for granted
- sleeping with your best friend
- saving up for a Yakuza hitman
- self-harming with a plastic fork
- applying for a restraining order
- the subject of a Channel 4 documentary into the world's most incompatible partners

I've been reflecting on our time together, how I feel now and what I really want from life. After this in-depth introspection I've decided I don't want to see you ever again because _____

Choose from:
- I'm still working through the strong feelings I have for my dad.
- I'm still working through the strong feelings I have for *your* dad.
- you have personal hygiene issues that make a relationship not just impossible but very yucky.
- you have more baggage than Terminal 5 at Heathrow.
- this is not so much a relationship as a prison sentence.
- I found those texts from the STI-ridden whore you've been seeing behind my back.
- you don't satisfy me sexually, or in any other way I can think of.
- I want to have sex with as many different people as I can.
- we don't share the same values. I'm a committed Christian while you worship Beelzebub.
- I can't deal with dating someone who looks like Oliver Hardy's fatter brother.
- you love showtunes more than me.
- there are no words that can adequately sum up the intense and bitter hatred I feel towards you.
- the voices in my head are saying, 'use the axe... use the axe...'

It is said that you get the partner you deserve. If this is the case I'm sure you'll end up living with _____

Choose from:
- the dimmest Kardashian
- a weasel
- toxic waste
- an inlatable love doll
- yourself
- a schizoid nutjob
- a materialistic, self-obsessed narcissist
- someone of the same gender
- a hobbit
- absolutely no one
- chlamydia

In conclusion, knowing this relationship is now officially and unconditionally over makes me feel like _____

Choose from:
- dancing.
- an elephant carrying an anvil on its back has suddenly been lifted from my shoulders.
- binge drinking.
- I'm born again.
- Nelson Mandela when he walked free.
- the curse has been lifted.
- skywriting 'Fuck You'.

Yours,

[ADD NAME]

P.S _____

Choose from:
- I was faking it every time.
- I hope you OD on your Botox.
- You stink 'down there'.
- It's barely four inches, let alone six.

65

Being pushed down a well by your mother-in-law

Mother-in-laws can be annoying, self-opinionated, highly judgmental and, above all, unpredictable. One day you're out for a leisurely stroll after a family Sunday lunch and the next thing you know you're lying unconscious at the bottom of a well. Knowing how to escape before a rising water table threatens to drown you is important, but more crucial is understanding how to deal with the situation afterwards.

Although it's tempting to just laugh off this episode for fear of embarrassment and awkwardness, ignoring it will only lead to festering resentment and possibly another attack on your life.

After you recover from your injuries it's important that you confront your mother-in-law as soon as possible about the attack and resolve your differences. Your aim should be turning what was attempted murder into an amusing anecdote that can be recounted at future family events, or in the Christmas round robin.

TIPS FOR MOTHER-IN-LAW CONFLICT RESOLUTION

Face the conflict head-on
The worst thing you can do is to ignore the situation and hope it goes away. It won't. By her actions, your mother-in-law is making a clear public statement about her relationship with you. This time she pushed you down a well. Next time she might stab you in the back (and not in the idiomatic sense).

Express your feelings to your spouse
Let your wife or husband know that being pushed down the well was hurtful, and not just on a physical level. It's important that your spouse supports you and doesn't laugh the whole incident off as some sort of silly prank or just a long-standing family tradition.

Detach yourself emotionally
To have a rational and objective discussion with your mother-in-law, it's important you enter the discussion on equal terms, i.e. see her as an acquaintance and not some form of substitute parent. That means not calling her 'mum' or 'mother' but instead using another name you both feel comfortable with. While it's very tempting to use 'mumzilla' or 'Mussolini in a skirt', addressing her by her first name or as Mrs _____ is the usual convention.

Use 'I' statements
'I' statements are more emotional and essential in getting your mother-in-law to understand your side of the story, whereas 'You' statements can make her feel under attack and therefore much more defensive. For example:

<u>Good</u>
'I feel sad that you had to resort to violence to show your true feelings towards me.'
<u>Bad</u>
'You nearly killed me, you fucking bitch!'

Be firm, not rude
During your discussions it will be extremely difficult to resist name-calling or cursing. If you feel the urge to say something vicious and insulting to your mother-in-law, take a deep breath and wait until you feel calm, or alternatively take a short break. This is far better than saying something you'll regret later, such as, 'Do you know the two worst things about you? Your faces.'

Work out the source of the tension
Why does your mother-in-law want you to die? The reason might have a foundation in truth, i.e. you're actually a lazy son of a bitch or an obvious gold digger. Other reasons might be completely irrational – you're ginger or she doesn't like your aura. The conflict can only be resolved when both of you understand the cause of her hatred (no matter how psycho she might seem).

Agree to change, or agree to disagree
Depending on the reasons above there might be a way you can modify your behaviour so while you'll never be wholly accepted by your mother-in-law, she agrees to tolerate you at least. If, however, her reasons are completely irrational then all you can do is walk away from the discussion and find a way to move on.
Note: This might literally mean moving.

Forgiving her is not a sign of weakness
If you're able to forgive someone who broke your collarbone and both your ankles, then be proud of yourself for having such a strong character. Showing such compassion also means she'll still be able to babysit next Friday night.